The Baseball Book
Of Lists

It all began when Alexander Cartwright made up the first list of baseball rules in 1845. Ever since, for better or for worse, baseball more than any other sport has abounded with lists and list-makers.

It is a game within itself and everybody plays it—from players (Joe DiMaggio, Rod Carew) to President (Ronald Reagan) to writers and announcers (Furman Bisher, Ernie Harwell) to managers (Walter Alston) to fans (Pete Enich).

They are all here in *The Baseball Book of Lists,* brought to you by popular demand of the readers who made best-sellers out of *The Book of Sports Lists* #1, #2 and #3.

The attributed lists are authentic. Others are the creation of the editors, who scoured the dugouts, the bullpens, the pressboxes, the clubhouses and the bleachers of America in search of an all-star lineup of lists.

We hope there will be a second *Baseball Book of Lists,* and we invite you, the reader, to participate. Send your list to:

Associated Features
370 Lexington Ave.
New York, NY 10017

Also by Phil Pepe and Zander Hollander:

THE BOOK OF SPORTS LISTS
THE BOOK OF SPORTS LISTS #2
THE BOOK OF SPORTS LISTS #3

THE BASEBALL BOOK OF LISTS

BY PHIL PEPE AND ZANDER HOLLANDER

An Associated Features Book

PINNACLE BOOKS NEW YORK

Acknowledgments

The editors formed the battery, but without the supporting team there would be no *Baseball Book of Lists*. We thank everybody who contributed a list and, in particular, these designated hitters who did more than a turn at bat: Eric Compton, L. Robert Davids, Bill Gallo, Red Foley and Frank Kelly.

EDITORS' NOTE: They are alphabetical and not necessarily in order of preference.

P.P. and Z.H.

THE BASEBALL BOOK OF LISTS

Copyright © 1983 by Associated Features Inc.

Some of the material herein was previously published in The Book of Sports Lists #1, #2, #3.

An original Pinnacle Books edition, published for the first time anywhere.

First printing, June 1983

ISBN: 0-523-41869-8

Printed in the United States of America

PINNACLE BOOKS, INC.
1430 Broadway
New York, N.Y. 10018

Several years ago, when we were accumulating material for *The Book of Sports Lists,* one of the people we asked to contribute a list was our old buddy from the Boston *Globe,* Ray Fitzgerald. Fitz was only too happy to help out. Not only that, he gave us support and encouragement and asked us not to forget him if we did a sequel. We didn't forget him, and Fitz didn't fail us. He appeared in *The Book of Sports Lists #2* and *The Book of Sports Lists #3* and he appears in *The Book of Baseball Lists.* His lists can be found on page 151 and 199.

About a year ago, Ray Fitzgerald suffered serious health problems that forced him to stop writing his column for the *Globe.* But he came through with a list for us. We think he dictated it to his wife, or one of his children.

When his list arrived, we called Ray to thank him and to see how he was doing. He was in a wheel chair. A stroke had left him partially paralyzed on the right side of his body. He couldn't type and that meant he was unable to knock out the brilliant, humorous columns he had turned out daily for his paper. But he said he was going to fight hard and he vowed he would be back. He also wished us luck with our latest project and said he was looking forward to receiving his copy of the book.

Unfortunately, Ray will never see it. He passed away a few weeks after we talked. We want his family to have this book, dedicated to Ray Fitzgerald.

Ray Fitzgerald, the gentlest, kindest of men, never complained about his own problems and was always solicitous of others. He made occasional visits to Boston a joy because of his good nature and wonderful sense of humor. We will miss him dearly.

Phil Pepe and Zander Hollander

CONTENTS

I   THE BABE, THE BIBLE AND THE BARD

II   DREAM TEAMS

III   AT THE BAT

IV   THE HUMAN COMEDY

V   A LEVEL OF GREATNESS

VI   THE TOUGHEST AND THE WORST

VII ON THE MOUND

VIII THROUGH THE AGES

IX   PLAYING ANOTHER GAME

X   THE LONG AND THE SHORT

XI   A MANNER OF SPEAKING

XII HALL OF FAME

XIII NAME-CALLING

XIV THE HOT STOVE LEAGUE

I

The Babe, The Bible and The Bard

9 Great Baseball Letters, Some of Which Made History

1. Dixie Walker was one of the most popular Brooklyn Dodgers—known as "The Peepul's Cheerce." In 1947, when Jackie Robinson was about to break the color line as a rookie, Walker was accused of being the ringleader for a group of Dodgers who resisted Branch Rickey's signing of Robinson. Walker denied the charge in a meeting with Rickey, who had made the accusation. A few days later, Walker wrote the following letter to the Dodger president.

March 26, 1947

Dear Mr. Rickey:
Recently the thought has occurred to me that a change of ball clubs would benefit both the Brooklyn ball club and myself. Therefore I would like to be traded as soon

as a deal can be arranged. My association with you, the
people of Brooklyn, the press and radio has been very
pleasant, and one I can truthfully say I am sorry has to
end.

For reasons I don't care to go in to, I feel my
decision is best for all concerned.

Very truly yours,
Dixie Walker

As it turned out, Walker didn't get traded until
the following year. Along the way he developed a
deep respect for Robinson and all he had to contend
with. And he was one of the first players to congratulate Robinson when he was named Rookie of the
Year.

2. and 3. Jackie Robinson's landmark career came to an
end when the Brooklyn Dodgers "traded" him to the
New York Giants after the 1956 season. He never
played another game. Buzzie Bavasi, a Dodger vice
president, gave Jackie his formal notice and owner
Walter O'Malley added his regrets.

Dear Jackie:

Enclosed herewith please find your Official Release
Notice indicating your assignment to the New York
Giants. This is something I never thought I would ever
have to do, and as a matter of fact, I want you to know
it was done with a great deal of reluctance.

Some time ago, I believe just before the season
started, you wrote me a letter which I still have in the
files. I appreciated that letter, just as I appreciated
everything you did for us both on and off the field. I
want to put this in writing, that you were a great deal of
assistance in our scouting . . . on numerous occasions
you helped us sign boys whom we would have lost.
There is a great deal more to baseball than just playing
the game on the field. I think you know what I
mean.

I certainly enjoyed our association over the past six
years, and I hope we can continue that association.

Please remember me to Rachel and to you both, our
door is always open.

Sincerely,
E. J. Bavasi
Vice President

The rookie, Jackie Robinson, with the Mahatma, Branch Rickey.

UPI

Dear Jackie and Rachel:

I do know how you and the youngsters must have
felt. It was a sad day for us, as well.

You were courageous and fair and philosophical on
radio and television and in the press. It was better that
way.

The roads of life have a habit of recrossing. There
could well be a future intersection. Until then, my best
to you both.

With a decade of memories,

Au Revoir,
Walter O'Malley

4. After World War II began, there was uncertainty as to whether major league baseball would continue. President Franklin D. Roosevelt provided the answer when he wrote what would forever be known as "The Green Light Letter" early in 1942. It was written to Baseball Commissioner Kenesaw Mountain Landis.

THE WHITE HOUSE
Washington

January 15, 1942

My dear Judge:

Thank you for yours of January fourteenth. As you will, of course, realize, the final decision about the baseball season must rest with you and the Baseball Club owners—so what I am going to say is solely a personal view and not an official point of view.

I honestly feel that it would be best for the country to keep baseball going. There will be fewer people unemployed and everybody will work longer hours and harder than ever before.

And that means that they ought to have a chance for recreation and for taking their minds off their work even more than before.

Baseball provides a recreation which does not last over two hours or two hours and a half, and which can be got for very little cost. And, incidentally, I hope that night baseball can be extended because it gives an opportunity to the day shift to see a game occasionally.

As to the players themselves, I know you agree with me that individual players who are of active military or naval age should go, without question, into the services. Even if the actual quality of the teams is lowered by the greater use of older players, this will not dampen the popularity of the sport. Of course, if any individual has some particular aptitude in a trade or profession, he ought to serve the

Government. That, however, is a matter which I know you can handle with complete justice.

Here is another way of looking at it—if 300 teams use 5,000 or 6,000 players, these players are a definite recreational asset to at least 20,000,000 of their fellow citizens—and that in my judgment is thoroughly worthwhile. With every best wish,

Very sincerely yours,

Franklin D. Roosevelt

Hon. Kenesaw M. Landis
333 North Michigan Avenue
Chicago, Illinois

5. Ring Lardner, a Chicago journalist who became one of the world's great short story writers, was an American original in the tradition of Poe, Whitman and Twain. A baseball fanatic, he wrote some of his early fiction about a sports hero, Jack Keefe, in the form of *A Busher's Letters,* in *The Saturday Evening Post.* They were collected in a book, *You Know Me Al,* published by Charles Scribner's Sons in 1916, from which the following is taken.

Yuma, Arizona, April 1

Dear Old Al: Just a line to let you know we are on our way back East. This place is in Arizona and it sure is sandy. They haven't got no regular ball club here and we play a pick-up team this afternoon. Callahan told me I would have work. He says I am using you because we want to get through early and I know you can beat them quick. That is the first time he has said anything like that and I guess he is wiseing up that I got the goods.

We was talking about the Athaletics this morning and Callahan say None of you fellows pitch right to Baker. I was talking to Lord and Scott afterward and I say Scott How do you pitch to Baker? He says I just use my fadeaway. I says How do you throw it? He says Just like you throw a fast ball to anybody else. I says Why do you call it a fadeaway then? He says Because when I throw it to Baker it fades away over the fence.

This place is full of Indians and I wish you could see them Al. They don't look nothing like the Indians we seen in that show last summer.

Your old pal,
Jack

6. As president of the American League, an irate Ban Johnson struck out the mighty Babe Ruth.

Chicago, Ill., June 21, 1922

Mr. George H. Ruth
% Brunswick Hotel
Boston, Mass.

Dear Sir:

There is a period in the trend of affairs when forbearance ceases to be a virtue. In your struggling moments to regain your prestige in the ranks of your profession, much indulgence was shown you. This plainly you did not understand, and again have overreached the point of consideration and the hope of thoughts of those who tried to bring you into the line of usefulness and worthy endeavor.

I was keenly disappointed and amazed when I received Umpire Dinneen's report, recounting your shameful and abusive language to that official in the game at Cleveland last Monday.

Bill Dinneen was one of the greatest pitchers the game ever produced, and with common consent we hand to him today the just tribute. He is one of the cleanest and most honorable men baseball ever fostered.

The American League is a stern and unrelenting organization. It has a clear conception of its duty toward the public. Any departure from sportsmanship, fair play and decency will be sharply rebuked. Your conduct at Cleveland on Monday was reprehensible to a great degree—shocking to every American mother who permits her boy to go to a professional game.

The American League cares nothing for Ruth. The

individual player means nothing to the organization. When he steps on the ballfield he is subject to our control and discipline. It is a leading question as to whether it is permissible to allow a man of your influence and breeding to continue in the game. The evidence is at hand that you have willfully betrayed two of the most enterprising and indulgent club owners in the game.

Again you offended on Tuesday. You branded Umpire Dinneen as "yellow." This is the most remarkable declaration a modern ballplayer has made. Dinneen stands out in the history of the game as one of the most courageous players we have ever had. If you could match up to his standard you would not be in the trough you occupy today. A man of your stamp bodes no good in the profession.

I have a thorough knowledge of your misconduct where you dragged your teammates to a violation of club rules absolutely at variance with discipline and loyalty. What I have in my possession I will later submit to President Ruppert and Col. Huston.

It would be the height of folly to condone the things you have done. In the history of baseball there was never another player who drew the enormous salary your contract calls for this year. You are plainly not earning your money, and your prestige has sunk to a standard where you are of no particular value to the New York club.

Coupled with your misconduct on Monday, you doubled the penalty on Tuesday. You are hereby notified of your suspension for five (5) days without salary. It seems the period has arrived when you should allow some intelligence to creep into a mind that has plainly been warped.

I am

Yours truly,
B. B. Johnson

7. When he was 18, he was the most famous batboy in the major leagues. Author of a book, *Yankee Batboy,* and confidant of some of the greatest Yankees of all, Joe

Carrieri was with the Yankees through six world championship seasons, and today he's a lawyer. What follows is one of the letters he wrote home when he was on a road trip, a reward given the batboys in those days.

The Chase
St. Louis, Mo.

Dear Mom & Dad,

I went downtown today with Billy Martin. I bought myself a pair of shoes. I threw away the other pair. They were no good anymore. All that was wrong with them was the top part of the shoe. It came off. I have $25 left. Casey Stengel said if I run short, he'll give me a check for $20. He doesn't want me to spend it foolishly, so he'd rather give it to me when I get home. That makes sense, I'm sure you'll agree.

We'll be out of this hotbox of a city tonight, and it can't come too soon. They've been talking about the Browns moving to Baltimore. I hear that's a hot city, too, but it can't be as hot as St. Louis.

I can't wait to get to Washington. That'll mean I'm that much closer to home.

Love,
Joe

8. Ira Berkow was sports editor of *Newspaper Enterprise Association* when he wrote to Casey Stengel, proposing they do a book together. This was Casey's answer.

Ira Berkow
Sports Editor
NEA Newspaper
N.Y. City: N.Y.

Dear Ira:

Your conversations, and the fact you were the working writer were inthused with the Ideas was great but frankly do not care for the great amount of work for myself.

Sorry but am not interested. Have to many proposi-
tions otherwise for this coming season.

Fact cannot disclose my future affairs.

Good Luck,

Casey Stengel,

N.Y. Mets & Hall of Famer

9. Shufflin' Phil Douglas, righthanded pitcher for the Giants
   in 1922, was 32 years old and in his ninth season. He
   was 11-4 when his longtime unquenchable thirst put
   him on yet another bender. Upon returning to the Polo
   Grounds he was "eaten out" by John McGraw and in
   his drunken stupor sat down and, on Giants' stationery,
   wrote the following note to outfielder Les Mann of the
   Cardinals, then in second place behind the Giants.

   Dear Les: I want to leave here. I don't want to see
   this guy (McGraw) win the pennant. You know that I
   can pitch and I am afraid that if I stay I will win the
   pennant for them. Talk this over with the boys, and if it
   is all right, send the goods to my house at night and I
   will go to the fishing camp. Let me know if you all
   want to do this and I will go home on the next train.

   Phil Douglas

   Douglas and Mann had been teammates on the Cubs
   in 1918. Mann, who was a YMCA guy, turned the
   letter over to then Cardinals' manager Branch Rickey
   who, in turn, contacted Judge Landis. On August 15, a
   couple of days after the letter was written, the Giants
   left for Pittsburgh and the next day were met in the
   Schenley Hotel by Landis. He confronted Douglas with
   the evidence and when Shufflin' Phil admitted he'd
   authored it, Landis promptly banned him from baseball
   for life. The Giants went on to win the pennant and the
   World Series that year.

Ted Patterson's 13 Television and Radio Firsts in Baseball

Ted Patterson is a Baltimore sportscaster and historian of sports broadcasting. He has written extensively about the history of radio and television in sports.

1. First Game Ever Broadcast—August 5, 1921. Pirates beat the Phillies, 8-0, with Harold Arlin announcing from Forbes Field over KDKA, Pittsburgh.
2. First Team to Air Games On a Daily Basis—1924 Chicago Cubs with Hal Totten on WMAQ.
3. First World Series Broadcast—1921, Giants vs. Yankees in the Polo Grounds, with Grantland Rice describing the action through telephone on three-station hook-up, WJZ, KDKA and WBZ.
4. Graham McNamee's First World Series Broadcast— 1923 on station WEAF. McNamee relieved sportswriter Bill McGeehan in Game 3, fourth inning. He became the voice of the golden age of sports.
5. First Night Game Broadcast—May 24, 1935. Reds vs. Phillies at Crosley Field. Red Barber announcing on WLW.
6. First Telecast—May 17, 1939. Princeton beats Columbia, 2-1, at Baker Field, Manhattan. Bill Stern announces on W2XBS.
7. First Major League Telecast—August 26, 1939, at Ebbets Field, Brooklyn. Dodgers vs. Reds. Red Barber was the announcer.
8. First Player-Turned Announcer—Jack Graney, former Cleveland outfielder, announced Indians' games from 1932 through 1954.
9. First to Announce on Regular Basis in New York— Red Barber, Dodgers, 1939.
10. First Night World Series Telecast—October 13, 1971, Pirates vs. Orioles at Pittsburgh. Pirates 4,

Graham McNamee, one of the pioneer broadcasters, interviews Babe Ruth at Yankee Stadium.

NBC-Ted Patterson Collection

    Orioles 3, with Curt Gowdy describing the action on NBC-TV.

11. First Baseball on Satellite to Europe—Cubs-Phils, 1961, at Wrigley Field. Two minutes of action; Jack Brickhouse and Vince Lloyd the announcers.

12. First TV Game in Chicago—April 20, 1946, WBKB. Cards at Cubs, Whispering Joe Wilson the announcer.

13. First Broadcaster to Use Phrase "Holy Cow."—No, it wasn't Harry Caray or Phil Rizzuto. It was the late Halsey Hall on Minneapolis Miller broadcasts in 1934.

All-Hollywood Baseball Team

1b—Gary Cooper as Lou Gehrig ("Pride of the Yankees").
2b—Frank Lovejoy as Rogers Hornsby ("The Winning Team").
3b—Jackie Robinson as Jackie Robinson ("The Jackie Robinson Story").
ss—Anthony Perkins as Jim Piersall ("Fear Strikes Out").

lf—Burt Lancaster as Jim Thorpe ("Jim Thorpe, All-American").

cf—Mickey Mantle as Mickey Mantle ("Safe at Home").

rf—William Bendix as Babe Ruth ("The Babe Ruth Story").

c—Paul Winfield as Roy Campanella ("It's Great to Be Alive").

p—Ronald Reagan as Grover Cleveland Alexander ("The Winning Team").

SOURCE: *The Washington Star*

7 Baseball Players Who Married Actresses or Entertainers

1. Joe DiMaggio   (Marilyn Monroe)
2. Lefty Gomez   (June O'Dea)
3. Don Rudolph   (Patti Waggin)
4. Andy Carey   (Lucy Marlowe)
5. Leo Durocher   (Laraine Day)
6. Rube Marquard   (Blossom Seeley)
7. Don Hoak   (Jill Corey)

Ronald Reagan's 3 Greatest Baseball Movies

1. "The Winning Team."
2. "Pride of the Yankees."
3. "The Stratton Story."

Says Mr. Reagan: "It's only coincidence that I played Old Alex himself (Grover Cleveland Alexander) in 'The Winning Team.'"

Long before he moved into the White House, Mr. Reagan was a sportscaster, broadcasting the games of the Iowa Oaks for a radio station in Des Moines, Iowa, and recreating the games of the Chicago Cubs. The following is his favorite baseball story:

"I don't think a single incident in any of the games I

A marriage made in Hollywood: Marilyn Monroe and Joe DiMaggio.

UPI

broadcast as a sports announcer impressed me so much as the last few weeks of the 1935 National League season. The Cubs came to a point where their only mathematical chance for winning the pennant lay in winding up the season, 21 games, without a defeat.

"As the totals started to mount, and they reached 15, then 16, without a defeat, you just couldn't believe it would happen. They went on and finished the season winning the last 21 games without a break. This, I believe, certainly was the biggest and most sustained thrill I ever had in broadcasting."

Phil Rizzuto's 15 Favorite Baseball Movies

Former Yankee shortstop great and current Yankee broadcaster and telecaster Phil Rizzuto is a dyed-in-the-celluloid movie buff. He thinks nothing of going to an afternoon movie before a night game on the road, then sitting up until the wee hours watching old movies on television, often seeing as many as five or six movies in a day. During one 10-day road trip, Rizzuto says he caught Alfred Hitchcock's "North By Northwest" seven times. Needless to say, it is one of his favorite non-baseball movies.

1. "Pride of the Yankees"—Gary Cooper, Teresa Wright, Walter Brennan
2. "Elmer The Great"—Joe E. Brown
3. "Alibi Ike"—Joe E. Brown
4. "The Monty Stratton Story"—James Stewart, June Allyson
5. "The Pride of St. Louis" (Dizzy Dean)—Dan Dailey, Joanne Dru
6. "Damn Yankees"—Tab Hunter, Ray Walston, Gwen Verdon
7. "Take Me Out To The Ball Game"—Frank Sinatra, Gene Kelly, Jules Munshin
8. "Bang The Drum Slowly"—Robert DeNiro, Michael Moriarty, Vincent Gardenia
9. "Angels In The Outfield"—Paul Douglas, Keenan Wynn, Janet Leigh
10. "The Jackie Robinson Story"—Jackie Robinson, Ruby Dee
11. "The Winning Team" (Grover Cleveland Alexander) —Ronald Reagan, Doris Day, Frank Lovejoy
12. "The Bad News Bears"—Walter Matthau, Tatum O'Neal
13. "It Happens Every Spring"—Ray Milland, Jean Peters, Paul Douglas
14. "Fear Strikes Out" (Jimmy Piersall)—Tony Perkins, Karl Malden, Norma Moore

Ronald Reagan played Grover Cleveland Alexander in "The Winning Team." Between innings at the studio, he's with the real Mrs. Alexander.

UPI

15. "Safe At Home"—Mickey Mantle, Roger Maris, Don Collier

Note: Aside from the obvious reason, Rizzuto chose "Pride of the Yankees" as his first choice because he says it was the most authentic of all the baseball movies. "They used real ballplayers (Bill Dickey, Babe Ruth) and even the actors were believable as ballplayers. The baseball scenes were very realistic.'' Rizzuto says he liked movies such as "Take Me Out To The Ball Game'' and "It Happens Every Spring,'' because "they were fun and entertaining, even if they were not realistic.''

Robert DeNiro, left; Michael Moriarty, center, and Vincent Gardenia starred in "Bang the Drum Slowly.''

Paramount-Sports Photo Source

William Shakespeare's 15 Best Baseball Quotes (No Comedy of Errors)

Although baseball was not invented until 300 years after the Elizabethan era, one can find several references to it in the plays of William Shakespeare. There's no record of the Immortal Bard having played for the Avon Hotspurs, but the old boy seems to have been familiar with some of the jargon. Harvey Sabinson, Executive Director of the League of New York Theatres and Producers, Broadway's equivalent of the Commissioner's Office, is a B-plus student of Shakespeare, but he found these likely references to our national pastime while reading the Bard's complete works one night.

1. "Quick, quick, good hands."—Antony and Cleopatra, Act V, Scene 2
2. " 'Tis true: there's magic in the web of it."—Othello, Act III, Scene 4
3. "What tidings send our scouts? I prithee, speak." —Henry VI, Part 1, Act V, Scene 3
4. "Our bruised arms hung up for monuments."—Richard III, Act I, Scene 1
5. " 'Twas I won the wager, though you hit the white; And, being a winner, God give you good night!"—The Taming of the Shrew, Act V, Scene 2
6. "O, that I were a glove upon that hand . . ."— Romeo and Juliet, Act II, Scene 2
7. "O wall, full often hast thou heard my moans."— A Midsummer's Night's Dream, Act V, Scene 1
8. "If I were mad, I should forget my son, Or madly think a babe of clouts were he."—King John, Act III, Scene 4
9. ". . . and so I shall catch the fly your cousin in the latter end . . ."—Henry V, Act V, Scene 2
10. "Let them play. Play, sirs."—Henry IV, Part 2, Act II, Scene 4
11. "Out, I say."—Macbeth, Act V, Scene 1
12. "O hateful error."—Julius Caesar, Act I, Scene 3
13. "A hit, a very palpable hit."—Hamlet, Act V, Scene 2
14. "Double, double."—Macbeth, Act IV, Scene 1
15. ". . . who stand so much on the new form that they cannot sit at ease on the old bench?"—Romeo and Juliet, Act 2, Scene 4

13 Baseball Excerpts from the Bible

1. The lineup: "Every man of the Children of Israel shall pitch by their father's house; every man with his own standard." Numbers 2:2
2. The visiting team: "Then the Philistines came and pitched in Judah." Judges 15:19
3. The manager: "Do I need madmen, that have brought this fellow to play?" 1 Samuel 21:16
4. The umpire: "And all the people shouted with a great shout. Whether it be good or bad, she shall not alter it." Ezekial 3:11; Leviticus 27:10.12

5. The fly ball: "He sent many flies among them and they caught every one." Proverbs 78:45; 11 Samuel 2:15
6. The squeeze play: "Amen sacrificed and Noah went in." Proverb 19:18
7. The misplay: "Who can understand errors?" Proverb 19:13
8. The hit-and-run: "They ran as soon as he had stretched out his hand." John 8:19
9. The home run: "And Absolom went for a homer and Abner was beaten." 11 Samuel 16:22; Hosts 3.2
10. The baseball groupie: "Rebekah came out with her pitcher." Genesis 24:15
11. The pitcher: "They shall not pass." Numbers
12. The catcher: "Suffer not a man to pass." Judges 111; 28
13. The announcer: "Though they roar, yet they cannot pass." Jeremiah 1; 22

25 Baseball Players Who Have Endorsed Wheaties

1. Babe Ruth
2. Lou Gehrig
3. Dizzy Dean
4. Joe DiMaggio
5. Lefty Grove
6. Carl Hubbell
7. Bill Dickey
8. Joe Cronin
9. Jimmie Foxx
10. Frankie Crosetti
11. Mel Ott
12. Eddie Stanky
13. Bob Feller
14. Ted Williams
15. Hank Greenberg
16. Stan Musial
17. Lou Boudreau
18. Phil Rizzuto
19. Jackie Robinson
20. Hal Newhouser
21. Roy Campanella

SOURCE: Gene Bratsch, General Mills

The people at Wheaties spelled it "Jimmy" Foxx when the great slugger endorsed their product, but official baseball records list him as Jimmie Foxx.

Wheaties

George Lois' 6 Favorite Ad Campaigns Involving Baseball Stars

George Lois is the famous maverick art director who claims that his advertising agency, Lois Pitts Gershon, is the only one that offers athletic scholarships (the agency has fielded dazzling amateur softball and basketball teams). Lois is the youngest member of the Art Directors Hall of Fame, with hundreds of ad awards to his credit. But the passion of his life is, and always will be, sports.

He was raised in the Bronx and spent more time in Yankee Stadium than in school. Now, at age 50, he can be found on city playgrounds and gyms playing racehorse basketball and swinging from the heels in fast-pitch softball games. He was the pioneer adman in the use of superstar personalities in TV commercials.

When Joe Namath was having problems over his Bachelors 3, Lois used the scotch-drinking quarterback to sell Ovaltine to kids. Another Namath/Lois spot showed Joe Willie typing on an Olivetti as his admiring female boss asks him out to dinner. In a TV spot for a stock brokerage house, he had sad-eyed Joe Louis ask the question: "Edwards & Hanly, where were you when I needed you?"

Lois is also known for his controversial *Esquire Magazine* covers of the '60s, including mean Sonny Liston as the first black Santa, and Muhammad Ali as the martyr St. Sebastian, a work of graphic iconography that protests, better than 1,000 words, the stripping of Ali's title for refusing to serve in the Viet Nam war.

1. The Most Tearful Spot Ever Made—The greatest sports heroes of their time (1967) appeared in one commercial in which they all cried for Maypo cereal. A decade before the Lite Beer "discovery" of sports personalities en masse, I conned Mickey Mantle, Willie Mays, Oscar Robertson, Wilt Chamberlain, Johnny Unitas, Ray Nitschke and Don Meredith to weep out the line, "I want my Maypo," as glycerine tears rolled down their cheeks.

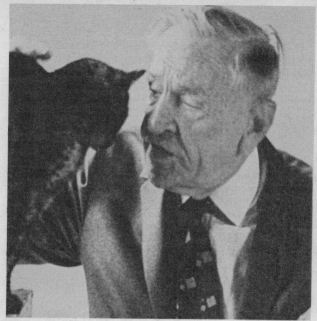

The Professor and the Pussy.
George Lois Collection

2. The Most Stengelese Delivery in Advertising—In a Casey Stengel TV lecture for Tabby cat food, the Ol' Professor, nose-to-nose with a pussycat, delivered his lines in machine-gun Stengelese, proving that all cat owners ain't sweet old ladies with scratches on their wrists. (And I swear the cat didn't understand a word Casey said.)

3. The Most Down Home Message—In a TV spot for stockbroker Edwards & Hanly in 1967, Mickey Mantle looked square in the camera and bared his soul:

"Boy, I'm telling you when I came up to the big leagues, I was a shufflin', grinnin', head-duckin' country boy. Well, I'm still a country boy, but I know a man down at Edwards & Hanly. I'm learnin'. I'm learnin'."

4. The Most Grandiose Baseball Dream/Scheme—In 1974, when nobody in America knew what a Subaru was, I persuaded the Japanese pitching ace Masaichi Kaneda to pitch the car. I filmed him in TV spots with Lou Brock, Gaylord Perry, Yogi Berra and Billy Martin—all telling their fellow Americans of the greatness of Kaneda. And, in sessions with the Baseball Commissioner's office, we plotted the first true World Series, between America's winning team and Japan's. But just as we were ready to spring the TV campaign, a new head man, who hated baseball, took over Subaru, and he kamikazied my master plan.

5. The Most Amazing Dialogue in a TV Spot—Another Lois masterpiece (1964) starred Yogi Berra selling Puss 'n Boots cat food. Yogi talked to the cat while the cat did fantastic exercises on the trampoline. Then, shot from behind, the cat talked up a blue streak, bobbing and weaving, as the Yog listened patiently. The voice of the cat, as any real baseball fan knew, was Yogi's batterymate Whitey Ford.

6. The Most Italian Opening Day Announcement—I created a newspaper ad for Trattoria, a New York Italian restaurant. It ran on Opening Day of the 1964 baseball season, with a baseball lineup that has been unmatched, before or since, for its molto Italian accent.

Yogi Berra charms the cat.

George Lois Collection

Bill Gallo's 9 "Baseball Figures I Have Drawn the Most"

Award-winning cartoonist Bill Gallo of the New York *Daily News* has an eye for faces. Over the years, he has depicted every major baseball personality in his inimitable style, but several individuals have popped up most frequently in Gallo cartoons because of their achievements or their physical characteristics.

1. Casey Stengel
2. Reggie Jackson
3. Leo Durocher
4. Billy Martin
5. Henry Aaron
6. Yogi Berra
7. Mickey Mantle
8. Pete Rose
9. Sandy Koufax
10. George Steinbrenner

Note: Steinbrenner rates special mention by Gallo, who has had great fun with the Yankee owner by depicting him as "General Von Steingrabber," a Teutonic military leader complete with helmet and German accent. Rather than take offense at Gallo's characterization, Steinbrenner has been amused by the cartoons and has requested several originals from the artist.

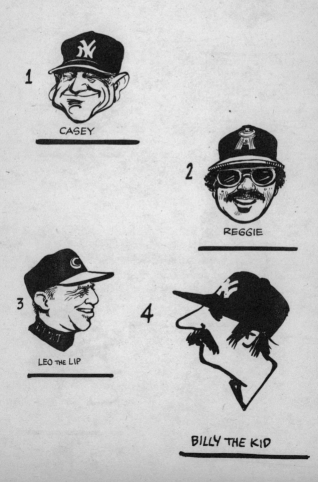

1

CASEY

2

REGGIE

3

LEO THE LIP

4

BILLY THE KID

5

HAMMERIN' HENRY

6

YOGI

7

MICKEY M.

8

PETE
ROSE

9

SANDY "K"

DH

STEINGRABBER

Panamanian-born Rod Carew grew up in New York City.

California Angels/Sports Photo Source

II

Dream Teams

L. Robert Davids' All-Time Foreign-Born, Short-Name and Long-Name Teams

As a boy on a farm in northern Iowa, L. Robert Davids listened to the Chicago Cubs' broadcasts of an announcer named Ronald Reagan. Davids grew up to become the founding father of the Society for American Baseball Research (SABR).

All-Foreign-Born

1b—John Anderson, Norway
2b—Rod Carew, Panama
3b—Aurelio Rodriguez, Mexico
 ss—Luis Aparicio, Venezuela
 of—Minnie Minoso, Cuba
 of—Elmer Valo, Czechoslavakia
 of—Bobby Thomson, Scotland
 c—Jimmy Archer, Ireland

p—Juan Marichal, Dominican Republic
p—Ferguson Jenkins, Canada
p—Bert Blyleven, Holland

All-Short-Name

1b—Lee May
2b—Ron Hunt
3b—Ron Cey
 ss—Tim Foli
of—Mel Ott
of—Sam Rice

Canadian-born Fergie Jenkins was a young Cub in 1967 when he struck
out six batters in three innings in the All-Star Game.

UPI

of—Pete Fox
c—Ed Ott
p—Bill Lee
p—Joey Jay
p—Jim Kaat

All-Long-Name

1b—Marv Throneberry
2b—Gene DeMontreville
3b—Billy Grabarkewitz
ss—Rabbit Maranville
of—Carl Yastrzemski
of—Frenchy Bordagaray
of—George Van Haltren
c—Ossee Schreckengost
p—Fritz Ostermueller
p—Ken Raffensberger
p—Fernando Valenzuela

Fernando Valenzuela has a long stride to match a long name.

Richard Pilling

Red Foley's All-Time All-Star Team of Players Who Never Played a Day in the Minor Leagues

First base—Ernie Banks, Frank Chance
Second base—Frank Frisch
Third base—Bob Horner, Eddie Yost
Shortstop—Dick Groat, Jack Barry
Outfield—Dave Winfield, Mel Ott, Al Kaline, Ethan Allen
Catcher—Michael (King) Kelly
Pitchers—Sandy Koufax, Johnny Antonelli, Bob Feller,
         Ted Lyons, Eppa Rixey, Eddie Plank, Jack Coombs,
         Catfish Hunter

Adds Foley: "Walter Johnson pitched one inning for Newark, whom he was managing in 1928 after he'd finished as a major leaguer. 'King' Kelly, star of the 1880s, was a noted catcher who broke into the NL without benefit of minor league training. He began with Cincinnati in 1878 and didn't go to the minors until 1894. He died in November, 1894. By '94, he'd drunk himself out of the National League. He eventually was elected to the Hall of Fame."

All-Time National and American League Teams

In the summer of 1982, *The Sporting News* and BFV&L conducted a nationwide poll of fans to select their choices for the all-time teams of both major leagues. The teams selected were then to meet in a mythical, computerized game, called "The Greatest Baseball Game Never Played," and broadcast by Lindsey Nelson and Jack Buck on network radio.

National League

1b—Pete Rose
2b—Rogers Hornsby
3b—Mike Schmidt
 ss—Honus Wagner
 of—Willie Mays
 of—Hank Aaron
 of—Stan Musial
  c—Roy Campanella
  p—Sandy Koufax

American League

1b—Lou Gehrig
2b—Rod Carew
3b—Brooks Robinson
 ss—Phil Rizzuto
 of—Babe Ruth
 of—Ted Williams
 of—Ty Cobb
  c—Yogi Berra
  p—Whitey Ford

Ed Browalski's All-Time Polish-American Major League Team

Ed Browalski—"Big Ed" to his many friends—is founder and president of the National Polish-American Sports Hall of Fame. He has been on the baseball scene for over 30 years as sports columnist for the Detroit *Polish Daily News*.

1b—Ted Kluszewski
2b—Bill Mazeroski
3b—George (Whitey) Kurowski
 ss—Tony Kubek
 lf—Stan Musial

cf—Al Simmons
rf—Carl Yastrzemski
 c—Frank Pytlak
 p—Stan Coveleski

Brawny Ted Kluszewski hammered 279 home runs for the Polish-American team.

UPI

reserve infielders—Bill (Moose) Skowron, Cass Michaels, Hank Majeski, Ray Jablonski
reserve outfielders—Richie Zisk, Greg Luzinski, Tom Paciorek
reserve catcher—Stan Lopata
pitching staff—Ed Lopat, Steve Gromek, Phil Niekro, Hank Borowy, Joe Niekro, Ron Perranoski, Jim Konstanty, Frank Tanana
manager—Danny Ozark
coaches—Dick Tracewski, Johnny Lipon, John Goryl

Ray Keyes' All-Time Eastern League Team

Ray Keyes is sports editor and columnist for the Williamsport (Pa.) *Sun-Gazette*.

    1b—Dale Long, Williamsport and Binghamton
    2b—Bobby Richardson, Binghamton
    3b—Clell (Butch) Hobson, Bristol
    ss—Granny Hamner, Utica
    of—Johnny Groth, Williamsport
    of—Pete Reiser, Elmira
    of—Richie Ashburn, Utica
  rhp—Orie Arntzen, Albany
  lhp—Tom (Lefty) George, York
    c—Stan Lopata, Utica
 util—Don Manno, Hartford, Albany, Williamsport
 mgr—Frank Lucchesi, Williamsport, Reading

Bob Broeg's All-Time St. Louis Baseball Team

Man and boy, Bob Broeg has been watching St. Louis baseball for 56 years, the last four decades as sportswriter, sports columnist, sports editor and assistant to the publisher of the St. Louis *Post-Dispatch*. He not only picks his all-time team, but also presents a batting order of the players selected.

  1. Lou Brock, lf
  2. Frank Frisch, 3b

3. George Sisler, 1b
4. Rogers Hornsby, 2b
5. Stan Musial, rf
6. Chick Hafey, cf
7. Walker Cooper, c
8. Marty Marion, ss
9. Dizzy Dean and Bob Gibson, p

The Cardinals' Dizzy Dean won 30 games in 1934.

UPI

Maury White's All-Time Iowa-Born (with one Exception) Major League Baseball Team

Maury White, sports columnist for the Des Moines *Register,* is a fourth-generation Iowan in the newspaper business. If he didn't see all the Iowans on his list, you can bet his father or his grandfather did.

1b—Hal Trosky, aka Harold Arthur Troyavesky, Norway (Iowa). Hit 35 homers as a rookie for Cleveland in 1934 and 42 in 1936.

2b—Dick Green, Sioux City. A vital cog in Oakland's World Series titles in 1972, 1973 and 1974, and damn near became Series MVP one of those years without bothering to get any hits.

3b—Denis Menke, Algona (because Bancroft didn't have a hospital). Good man and 101 homers in a dozen years with Milwaukee, Atlanta, Houston and Cincinnati.

ss—Dave (Beauty) Bancroft, Sioux City. A Hall of Famer who played 16 seasons in the bigs and managed the Boston Braves in 1923-27.

lf—Fred Clarke, farm near Winterset. Another Hall of Famer. Hit .315 for life, once had four assists from left field and managed Pittsburgh for 13 years.

cf—Bing Miller, Vinton. Hit .312 in long AL career, mostly with Philadelphia Athletics in the Jimmie Foxx-Lefty Grove glory days.

rf—George Stone, Lost Nation. Hit .301 for Boston and the St. Louis Browns early in the century.

c—Hank Severeid, Story City. Batted .289 from 1911-1926 and played 10 seasons with the St. Louis Browns.

p—Rapid Robert Feller, righthander, Van Meter. Hall of Famer, 2,581 strikeouts for Cleveland. Traffic Circle in hometown named in his honor. If the town has a sense of history, the circle would have no speed limit.

p—Dazzy Vance, righthander, Orient. Had 197-140 career record and 2,045 Ks in long career with a number of teams, including 11 years as a Brooklyn Dodger. Also a Hall of Famer.

p—Urban (Red) Faber, righthander, Cascade. Was 254-212 in 20 years with the Chicago White Sox and won three games in the 1917 World Series. Another Hall of Famer.

p—Earl Whitehill, lefthander, Cedar Rapids. Was 218-185 in 17 years, mostly with Detroit. Was 22-8 in 1933.

p—Bob Locker, long reliever, George. In 576 games, mostly with the White Sox and A's, from 1965-1975 and never started one. Great sinker.

Iowan Bob Feller, right, meets up with Carl Hubbell at a 1937 spring training game in Rome, Georgia.

UPI

p—Eddie Watt, short relief, Lamoni. Had 10 seasons in the majors, mostly with Baltimore during some World Series years.

mgr—Adrian Constantine (Cap) Anson, aka Pop Anson, Marshalltown. First white child born in Marshall County. Hall of Fame. Hit .300 for 20 straight seasons, including .421 in 1887. One of the great early managers. Could be the third baseman except Menke is a helluva good guy and it's kind of nice picking a few who are still alive and breathing.

gm—Ed Barrow, the exception. Born in Illinois, moved to Des Moines as a baby and grew up here, once being circulation manager for an ancestor of the *Register*. Became a front office titan with the great Yankee teams of the '20s and '30s and is believed to be the man who changed Babe Ruth from part-time pitcher to full-time outfielder. Hall of Fame.

chaplain—William Ashley (Billy) Sunday, aka The Evangelist, Ames. Played eight seasons in the National League with Chicago and Pittsburgh, hit .243, then turned to full-time duty in the pulpit and became a famous evangelist, proving that nicknames sometimes do tell the story.

Doug Huff's All-Time Major League Team of West Virginians

1b—Dick Hoblitzell, 1908-18, Reds and Red Sox
2b—Bill Mazeroski, 1956-72, Pirates
3b—George Brett, 1973-active, Royals
ss—Jack Glasscock, 1879-95, eight teams
of—Jesse Burkett, 1890-1905, five teams, Hall of Famer
of—Earle (Greasy) Neale, 1916-24, Reds and Phillies, college and pro football Hall of Famer
of—Lewis (Hack) Wilson, 1923-34, four teams, born in Pennsylvania, but is buried in West Virginia, where he resided most of his adult life.

c—Steve Yeager, 1972-active, Dodgers; backup—Andy
Seminick, 1943-57, Phillies and Reds
   rhp—Lew Burdette, 1950-67, seven teams
   lhp—Wilbur Cooper, 1912-26, Pirates, Cubs, Tigers
   utility—Toby Harrah, 1969-active, three teams; Paul
Popovich, 1964-75, three teams; Gene Freese, 1955-66,
six teams; Larry Brown, 1963-74, four teams

Dave Newhouse's Major League All-Star Team of Players Who Grew Up in Oakland

Dave Newhouse is a sports columnist on the Oakland
Tribune.

   1b—Ferris Fain
   2b—Joe Morgan
   3b—Cookie Lavagetto
   ss—Bill Rigney
   of—Frank Robinson
   of—Vada Pinson
   of—Curt Flood
   c—Ernie Lombardi
   p—Ray Kremer
   p—Rudy May

Bernie Lincicome's All-Star Team of Players Born in Florida

   1b—Steve Garvey, Tampa
   2b—Dave Johnson, Orlando
   3b—Wayne Garrett, Sarasota
   ss—Woody Woodward, Miami
   of—Andre Dawson, Miami
   of—Lou Piniella, Tampa
   of—Hal McRae, Avon Park
   dh—Boog Powell, Lakeland

c—Zack Taylor, Yulee
p—Steve Carlton, Miami
mgr—Al Lopez, Tampa

Steve Garvey had his beginnings in Florida, where his dad drove the team bus for the Dodgers in spring training.

Nancy Hogue

Bernie Lincicome's All-Star Team of Players Who Died in Florida

1b—Jimmie Foxx, Miami, 1967
2b—Napoleon Lajoie, Daytona Beach, 1959
3b—Bill McKechnie, Bradenton, 1965

    ss—Joe Tinker, Orlando, 1948
    of—Max Carey, Miami Beach, 1976
    of—Heinie Manush, Sarasota, 1971
    of—Paul Waner, Sarasota, 1965
    dh—Joe Medwick, St. Petersburg, 1975
     c—Jimmie Wilson, Bradenton, 1947
     p—Ed Walsh, Pompano Beach, 1959
     p—Dazzy Vance, Homosassa Springs, 1961
  mgr—Burt Shotton, Lake Wales, 1962

Note: Lincicome, sports editor of the Fort Lauderdale
News, points out that of those who died in Florida, all are
in the Hall of Fame except Wilson and Shotton.

Pete Enich's All-Time Team of Players Born in Kansas

1b—George (Boots) Grantham, Galena. Batted .302 in
1,444 games, including 1,508 hits. Nickname derived from
leading NL in errors for several years.

2b—Joe Tinker, Muscotah. Hall of Fame. Immortalized
in Franklin P. Adams' poem. The double-play combo of
Tinker-Evers-Chance actually had only 54 DPs playing as
a unit, 1906-1909. Normally a shortstop, but played some
second base. Feuded with teammate Johnny Evers and
didn't speak to him for three years.

3b—Bob Horner, Junction City. One of baseball's top
power hitters, he hit 56 home runs in first 210 major
league games.

ss—Bill Russell, Pittsburg. Member of Dodgers' infield
that played together longer than any other infield in major
league history. All-State basketball player in high school.

of—Enos Cabell, Ft. Riley. Rangy former junior college
basketball star who had best years with Houston Astros.
Lifetime average .275 with more than 1,000 hits. Normally an infielder, Cabell has experience in the outfield.

of—Don Lock, Wichita. Brought up in the Yankee
organization, Lock had two outstanding years with the

Washington Senators (1963-64). A righthanded hitter, he hit more than half of his 122 career homers against right-handed pitching.

of—Dick Cooley, Leavenworth. Turn-of-the-century stalwart who rapped 1,582 hits for St. Louis, Philadelphia, Pittsburgh and Boston, despite batting seventh or eighth in the lineup. "Sir Richard" had a .295 lifetime average.

c—Josh Billings, Grantville. By virtue of longevity, Billings is the Wheat State's catcher. With Cleveland from 1913-1918, then St. Louis until 1923, Billings averaged nine hits a year, 2.7 RBI, no home runs, four runs scored and finished his career with a .217 batting average.

p—Walter Johnson, Humboldt. Hall of Fame. "The Big Train" spent his entire 21-year career with the lowly Washington Senators and still managed to win 416 games. Considered by many the greatest pitcher in history, Johnson won 20 games in 12 of his 21 seasons, striking out 3,508 hitters.

p—Mike Torrez, Topeka. Should approach 230 victories when his career is over. Major college potential as a basketball player at Topeka High in the early '60s.

p—Ray Sadecki, Kansas City. Winning pitcher in the first game of the 1964 World Series, Sadecki finished his career with the Mets in 1977. His career record was 135-131.

p—Rudy May, Coffeyville. Classy lefthander who seemingly got lost in the Steinbrenner shuffle after signing with the Yankees as a free agent in 1980.

relief—Neil Allen, Kansas City. Standout high school quarterback who signed a letter of intent with Kansas State in 1976. Opted for Mets and looms as one of Kansas' all-time best products.

mgr—Ralph Houk, Lawrence. Managed Yankees to three AL pennants, 1961-63, and after a stint as general manager, returned to lead the Bombers to a 10th-place finish in 1966. Also managed Detroit and Boston.

coach—Gene Mauch, Salina. Winningest of the Philadelphia Phillies' managers in modern times, with 646 victories from 1960 through 1968. Piloted Phillies to 23 consecutive defeats in 1961, the longest losing streak in the 20th century. Later managed Montreal, Minnesota, California.

coach—Bob Swift, Salina. Coached Detroit Tigers, Kansas City A's and Washington Senators. Interim manager Detroit, 1966. Played and coached at major league level 26 years.

coach—Don Gutteridge, Pittsburg. Rapped 148 hits as the starting second baseman for the AL champion St. Louis Browns in 1944. After coaching many years, he managed the Chicago White Sox in 1969-70.

umpire—George Magerkurth, McPherson. A giant of a man, 6-4, 230. Feisty NL umpire left a boxing career of more than 70 pro fights to become a big league umpire. Actually had more fights after becoming an umpire.

Walter Alston's All-Time
Dodger Team

Walter Alston was an unknown with only one major league at-bat when he was named to succeed Charlie Dressen as manager of the Brooklyn Dodgers in 1954. He signed a one-year contract and stayed with the Dodgers through 23 one-year contracts, winning over 2,000 major league games, more than any manager in history except Connie Mack, John McGraw, Joe McCarthy and Bucky Harris. He retired after the 1976 season and agreed to select his all-time Dodger team for *The Complete Handbook of Baseball*. It follows:

1b—Gil Hodges
2b—Jim Gilliam
3b—Jackie Robinson
ss—PeeWee Reese
lf—Sweet Lou Johnson
cf—Duke Snider
rf—Carl Furillo
c—Roy Campanella

p—Sandy Koufax
   Don Drysdale
   Don Sutton
   Don Newcombe
   Carl Erskine
   Clem Labine
   Ron Perranoski
   Jim Brewer

All-time Dodger Duke Snider swats a home run against the Pirates in 1961.

UPI

Russ Schneider's All-Time Cleveland Indians Good Guys and Not-So-Good Guys Team

Before he switched to the football Browns, good guy Russ Schneider covered the baseball Indians for the Cleveland *Plain Dealer* for 15 seasons. He restricts his selections to the players he covered on a regular basis.

Good Guys

1b—Fred Whitfield
2b—Duane Kuiper
3b—Max Alvis
 ss—Fred Stanley
of—Buddy Bell
of—Gomer Hodge
of—Chico Salmon
 c—Joe Azcue
dh—John Lowenstein
rhp—Eric Raich (my son-in-law)
lhp—Fritz Peterson and Rick Waits
relief—Bob Tiefenauer and Don McMahon
mgr—George Strickland

Not-So-Good-Guys

1b—Jim Gentile
2b—Pedro Gonzalez
3b—Luis Alvarado
 ss—Larvell Blanks
of—Alex Johnson
of—Jose Cardenal
of—George Hendrick
 c—John Romano
dh—Cliff Johnson
rhp—Wayne Garland
lhp—Don Hood
relief—Victor Cruz
mgr—Joe Adcock

Bill Parrillo's All-Time All-Star Baseball Team from Poor Little Rhode Island

A native of Rhode Island, Bill Parillo is sports columnist for the Providence *Journal*.

1b—Jack Flynn, Providence
2b—Napoleon Lajoie, Woonsocket

3b—Johnny Goryl, Cumberland
ss—Jimmy (Scoops) Cooney, Cranston
of—Hugh Duffy, Cranston
of—Johnny Cooney, Cranston
of—Joe Connolly, North Smithfield
dh—Davey Lopes, East Providence
 c—Gabby Hartnett, Woonsocket
 p—Andy Coakley, Providence
 p—Max Surkont, Central Falls
 p—Chet Nichols, Pawtucket
 p—Dave Stenhouse, Westerly

Gabby Hartnett, the son of a streetcar conductor who had 14 children,
went from Woonsocket, Rhode Island, to the majors.

UPI

p—Phil Paine, Chepachet
relief pitcher—Clem Labine, Lincoln
mgr—Eddie Sawyer, Westerly
gm—Roland Hemond, Central Falls, or Lou Gorman, Providence

Parrillo adds: "My team has three Hall of Famers (Hartnett, Lajoie, Duffy) and even comes equipped with its own umpires—Hank Soar, Pawtucket; Paul Pryor, Woonsocket; Bob Stewart, Cumberland; Jim Duffy, Pawtucket; and its own agents—Jerry Kapstein, Providence (Steve Garvey, Fred Lynn, Carlton Fisk, Joe Rudi, etc.) and Tony Pennacchia, Cranston (Jim Rice, Cecil Cooper, Butch Hobson, etc.).

"Did you know that the very first World Series was played in Rhode Island? In 1884, the Providence Grays of the National League met the New York Metropolitans of the American Association. The series was a result of an agreement signed by warring leagues to stop the raiding of players. It was a three-game series. Old Hoss Radbourne pitched all three victories for the champion Grays."

Baseball's All-Time Team of Players Born on April Fool's Day

1b—Willie Montanez, 1948
2b—Rod Kanehl, 1934
3b—Dick Kenworthy, 1941
ss—Murray Franklin, 1914
of—Rusty Staub, 1944
of—Claude Cooper, 1892
of—Jeff Heath, 1915
c—Bill Friel, 1876
rhp—Phil Niekro, 1939
lhp—Ron Perranoski, 1936
relief—Will McEnaney, 1952
mgr—Hugo Bezdek, 1884

Submitted by Barry Janoff

No April fool in the kitchen, Rusty Staub cooks up a storm at Rusty's, his New York restaurant.

UPI

Baseball's All-Time Team of Players
Born on New Year's Day

    1b—Hank Greenberg, 1911
    2b—Joe Martin, 1876
    3b—Tom Downey, 1884
    ss—Frank Connaughton, 1869
    of—Sherry Robertson, 1919
    of—Art Parks, 1911
    of—Ethan Allen, 1904
     c—Benny Meyer, 1888
   rhp—Carl Scheib, 1927
   lhp—Bob Owchinko, 1955
    dh—Lynn Jones, 1953
   mgr—Herman Franks, 1914

Submitted by Barry Janoff

Baseball's All-Time Team of Players
Born on Christmas Day

    1b—Walter Holke, 1892
    2b—Nellie Fox, 1927
    3b—Gene Robertson, 1899
    ss—Manny Trillo, 1950
    of—Rickey Henderson, 1958
    of—Jo Jo Moore, 1908
    of—Red Barnes, 1903
     c—Gene Lamont, 1946
   rhp—Ned Garver, 1925
   lhp—Alvin Jackson, 1935
 relief—Jack Hamilton, 1938
   mgr—Ben Chapman, 1908

Submitted by Barry Janoff

Laura Van Sant's Best-Looking Baseball Team

Beauty, of course, is in the eye of the beholder, but this is one young woman's idea of the best-looking baseball team. Ms. Van Sant is from Chapel Hill, N.C.

    1b—Lee Mazzilli
    2b—Doug Flynn
    3b—George Brett
    ss—Bucky Dent
    of—Lou Piniella
    of—Joe Charboneau
    of—Jesus Figueroa
     c—Marc Hill
     p—Charlie Liebrandt

Monte Irvin's All-Time Negro*
All-Star Team

    1b—Buck Leonard, Homestead Grays
    2b—Sammy T. Hughes, Baltimore Elite Giants
    3b—Ray Dandridge, Newark Eagles
    ss—Willie Wells, Newark Eagles
    lf—Martin Dihigo, New York Cubans
    cf—Cool Papa Bell, St. Louis Stars
    rf—Bill Wright, Baltimore Elite Giants
     c—Josh Gibson, Homestead Grays
    rhp—Satchel Paige, Kansas City Monarchs
    lhp—Slim Jones, Philadelphia Stars
    mgr—Rube Foster, Chicago American Giants

*"We were Negroes, then," says Hall of Famer Monte Irvin, who, long before he became a hero of the New York Giants, was a star of the Newark Eagles. They played in the Negro National and Negro American leagues, and Monte, mostly an infielder then, played in the league from 1937 through 1948 (with time out for Army duty in Europe

The Kansas City Royals' George Brett made Laura Van Sant's best-looking lineup.

UPI

Satchel Paige didn't get his chance to pitch in the majors until he was in his forties in 1948, when he posted a 6–1 record for the Cleveland Indians.

UPI

during World War II). Monte signed with the Giants for $5,000 in 1949. "I took a cut from what I was making at Newark," Monte says, "But it was time." The rest is history.

Baseball's All-Second-Generation Team

  1b—Todd Demeter (Don)
  2b—Bump Wills (Maury)
  3b—Buddy Bell (Gus)
  ss—Dale Berra (Yogi)
  of—Terry Francona (Tito)
  of—Jeff Pyburn (Jim)
  of—Terry Kennedy (Bob)
   c—Bob Boone (Ray)
 rhp—Matt Keough (Marty)
 lhp—Steve Trout (Dizzy)
utility—Vance Law (Vern)
  ph—Milt May (Pinky)

Note: All players were active in 1982 and on major league 40-man rosters in spring training. Father's name in parentheses.

III

At the Bat

11 Teammates Who Hit 40 or More Home Runs in a Single Season

1. Roger Maris (61), Mickey Mantle (54), New York Yankees, 1961 115
2. Babe Ruth (60), Lou Gehrig (47), New York Yankees, 1927 107
3. Babe Ruth (46), Lou Gehrig (46), New York Yankees, 1931 92
4. Babe Ruth (49), Lou Gehrig (41), New York Yankees, 1930 90
5. Ted Kluszewski (47), Wally Post (40), Cincinnati Reds, 1955. 87
6. Rocky Colavito (45), Norm Cash (41), Detroit Tigers, 1961 86
7. Orlando Cepeda (46), Willie Mays (40), San Francisco Giants, 1961 86
8. Johnny Bench (45), Tony Perez (40), Cincinnati Reds, 1970 85
9. Dave Johnson (43), Darrell Evans (41), Atlanta Braves, 1973 . . . . 84*

*Hank Aaron also hit 40 homers, the only time in major league history three players from the same team hit 40 home runs in a single season.

Roger Maris, left, and Mickey Mantle made a smashing duet in 1961.
UPI

10. Duke Snider (42), Roy Campanella (41), Brooklyn
    Dodgers, 1952 83
11. Carl Yastrzemski (40), Rico Petrocelli (40), Boston
    Red Sox, 1969 80

SOURCE: Donald L. Nelson, Member SABR

12 Sluggers Who Hit 60 or More Home Runs in a Single Season

	No.	Team	League	Year
1. Joe Bauman	72	Roswell	Longhorn	1954
2. Joe Hauser	69	Minneapolis	Amer. Assn.	1933
3. Bob Crues	69	Amarillo	West Texas-N.M.	1948
4. Dick Stuart	66	Lincoln	Western	1956
5. Bob Lennon	64	Nashville	Southern	1954
6. Joe Hauser	63	Baltimore	International	1930
7. Moose Clabaugh	62	Tyler	East Texas	1926
8. Ken Guettler	62	Shreveport	Texas	1956
9. Roger Maris	61	New York	American	1961
10. Babe Ruth	60	New York	American	1927
11. Tony Lazzeri	60	Salt Lake City	Pacific Coast	1925
12. Frosty Kennedy	60	Plainview	Southwest	1956

3 Players Who Won A Batting Crown without Hitting a Home Run

1. Clarence Beaumont, Pittsburgh, 1902
2. Zack Wheat, Brooklyn, 1918
3. Rod Carew, Minnesota, 1972

The 10 Toughest Home Run Areas in Major League History

1. Polo Grounds, center field
2. Old Yankee Stadium, center field
3. Forbes Field, center field
4. Los Angeles Coliseum, center field
5. Forbes Field, left field
6. Yankee Stadium, left field
7. Busch Stadium, any field
8. Oakland Coliseum, any field
9. Griffith Stadium, left field
10. Texas Stadium, right field

SOURCE: Red Foley

The 13 Easiest Home Run Areas in Major League History

1. Polo Grounds, right field
2. Baker Bowl, right field
3. Fenway Park, left field
4. Polo Grounds, left field
5. Ebbets Field, left field
6. League Park, right field
7. Los Angeles Coliseum, left field
8. Old Yankee Stadium, right field
9. Forbes Field, left field (''Kiner's Korner'')
10. Shibe Park, left field
11. Sportsman's Park, right field (with the screen down)
12. Atlanta Stadium, any field
13. Wrigley Field, any field (with the wind blowing out)

Note: Interestingly, Polo Grounds, New York; Ebbets Field, Brooklyn; League Park, Cleveland; L.A. Coliseum; Forbes Field, Pittsburgh; Baker Bowl and Shibe Park, Philadelphia; and Sportsman's Park, St. Louis, are no longer in existence. And Yankee Stadium has been remodeled.

SOURCE: Red Foley

25 Greatest Home Run Hitters of All Time Per 100 At-Bats (Through 1982)

		Home Runs per 100 ABs
1.	Babe Ruth	8.5
2.	Ralph Kiner	7.1
3.	Harmon Killebrew	7.0
4.	Dave Kingman	7.0
5.	Mike Schmidt	6.8
6.	Ted Williams	6.8
7.	Mickey Mantle	6.6
8.	Jimmie Foxx	6.6
9.	Hank Greenberg	6.4
10.	Willie McCovey	6.4
11.	Lou Gehrig	6.2
12.	Hank Aaron	6.1
13.	Willie Mays	6.1
14.	Willie Stargell	6.1
15.	Eddie Mathews	6.0
16.	Hank Sauer	6.0
17.	Reggie Jackson	6.0
18.	Frank Howard	5.9
19.	Frank Robinson	5.9
20.	Roy Campanella	5.8
21.	Rocky Colavito	5.8
22.	Gus Zernial	5.7
23.	Duke Snider	5.7
24.	Norm Cash	5.6
25.	Johnny Mize	5.6

Note: Minimum 4,000 at-bats.

SOURCE: National Baseball Hall of Fame and Museum

The Phillies' Mike Schmidt is in top five for home runs per 100 at-bats.
Nancy Hogue

The 8 Top Home Run Hitting Duos in Baseball History

Duo and Team	Total
1. Roger Maris (61), Mickey Mantle (54), New York Yankees, 1961	115
2. Babe Ruth (60), Lou Gehrig (47), New York Yankees, 1927	107
3. Hack Wilson (56), Gabby Hartnett (37), Chicago Cubs, 1930	93
4. Jimmy Foxx (58), Al Simmons (35), Philadelphia Athletics, 1932	93
5. Babe Ruth (46), Lou Gehrig (46), New York Yankees, 1931	92
6. Hank Greenberg (58), Rudy York (33), Detroit Tigers, 1938	91
7. Willie Mays (52), Willie McCovey (39), San Francisco Giants, 1965	91
8. Babe Ruth (49), Lou Gehrig (41), New York Yankees, 1930	90

SOURCE: Donald L. Nelson, SABR

All-Time Listing of the Top Home Run Hitters Whose Names Begin with Each Letter of the Alphabet, 1900-1982

A—Henry Aaron, 755
B—Ernie Banks, 512
C—Orlando Cepeda, 379
D—Joe DiMaggio, 361
E—Del Ennis, 288
F—Jimmy Foxx, 534
G—Lou Gehrig, 493
H—Frank Howard, 382
I—Monte Irvin, 99
J—Reggie Jackson, 464
K—Harmon Killebrew, 573

Willie Mays, left, MVP in 1965, and teammate Willie McCovey, MVP in 1969, combined for 91 homers in 1965. *UPI*

L—Greg Luzinski, 262
M—Willie Mays, 660
N—Graig Nettles, 313
O—Mel Ott, 511
P—Tony Perez, 363
Q—Jamie Quirk, 12
R—Babe Ruth, 714
S—Willie Stargell, 475
T—Frank Thomas, 286
U—Del Unser, 87
V—Mickey Vernon, 172
W—Ted Williams, 521
X—
Y—Carl Yastrzemski, 442
Z—Gus Zernial, 237

Note: There has never been a major league player whose last name began with the letter "X"; closest race was among the Cs, Cepeda (379) beating out Norm Cash (377) and Rocky Colavito (374).

Brothers Who Homered in the Same Game

1. Joe and Dom DiMaggio
2. Tony and Al Cuccinello
3. Wes and Rick Ferrell
4. Jose and Hector Cruz

Submitted by Brian McGill, Philadelphia, Pa.

Baseball's 20 Easiest Strikeouts
(Through 1982)

	At-Bats Per Strikeout
1. Dave Kingman	3.38
2. Reggie Jackson	3.93
3. Bobby Bonds	4.01

The DiMaggio boys in 1940: (left to right) Vince, Joe, Dominic.

4.	Mike Schmidt	4.01
5.	Rick Monday	4.06
6.	Dick Allen	4.07
7.	Donn Clendenon	4.08
8.	Willie Stargell	4.12
9.	Woodie Held	4.26
10.	Greg Luzinski	4.31
11.	Gene Tenace	4.42
12.	Frank Howard	4.44
13.	Larry Hisle	4.47
14.	Deron Johnson	4.51
15.	Jim Wynn	4.66
16.	Mickey Mantle	4.74
17.	Harmon Killebrew	4.80
18.	Lee May	4.85
19.	Bob Allison	4.87
20.	Jeff Burroughs	4.89

Note: Ratings based on 4,000 at-bats.

Baseball's 9 Toughest Strikeouts of All Time

		At-Bats Per Strikeout
1.	Joe Sewell	62.56
2.	Lloyd Waner	44.92
3.	Nellie Fox	42.92
4.	Tommy Holmes	40.92
5.	Andy High	33.85
6.	Sam Rice	33.71
7.	Frankie Frisch	33.50
8.	Frank McCormick	30.28
9.	Don Mueller	29.89

Note: Ratings are based on a minimum of 4,000 at-bats. Strikeout records were not kept prior to 1913, therefore records of Wee Willie Keeler, Lave Cross, Tris Speaker and Stuffy McInnis—who would make the top 9—are incomplete and not listed.

SOURCE: The Elias Baseball Bureau

Dave Kingman owns dubious strikeout honor.

Mitchell B. Reibel

21 Players Who Batted 1.000 for Their Major League Careers

1. Doc Bass, Boston (NL), 1918, one at-bat
2. Steve Biras, Cleveland, 1944, two at-bats
3. Bill Burns, Baltimore, 1902, one at-bat
4. Jackie Gallagher, Cleveland, 1923, one at-bat
5. Roy Gleason, Los Angeles (NL), 1963, one at-bat
6. Mike Hopkins, Pittsburgh, 1902, two at-bats
7. Steve Kuczek, Boston (NL), 1949, one at-bat
8. Chuck Lindstrom, Chicago (AL), 1958, one at-bat
9. Red Lutz, Cincinnati, 1922, one at-bat
10. John Mohardt, Detroit, 1922, one at-bat
11. Heinie Odom, New York (AL), 1925, one at-bat
12. Curley Onis, Brooklyn, 1935, one at-bat
13. John Paciorek, Houston, 1963, three at-bats
14. Bill Peterman, Philadelphia (NL), 1942, one at-bat
15. Ty Pickup, Philadelphia (NL), 1918, one at-bat
16. Fred Schemanske, Washington, 1923, two at-bats
17. Roe Skidmore, Chicago (NL), 1970, one at-bat
18. Tige Stone, St. Louis (NL), 1923, one at-bat
19. Allie Watt, Washington, 1920, one at-bat
20. Al Wright, Boston (NL), 1933, one at-bat
21. George Yantz, Chicago (NL), 1912, one at-bat

Note: Chuck Lindstrom is the son of Hall of Famer Freddie Lindstrom, and John Paciorek is the brother of major leaguer Tom Paciorek.

8 Players Who Batted in 6 Runs in 1 Inning

1. Fred Merkle, New York Giants, May 13, 1911, first inning.
2. Bob Johnson, Philadelphia Athletics, August 29, 1937, fifth inning.
3. Tom McBride, Boston Red Sox, August 4, 1945, fourth inning.
4. Joe Astroth, Philadelphia Athletics, September 23, 1950, sixth inning.

5. Gil McDougald, New York Yankees, May 3, 1951, ninth inning.
6. Sam Mele, Chicago White Sox, June 10, 1952, fourth inning.
7. Jim Lemon, Washington Senators, September 5, 1959, third inning.
8. Jim Ray Hart, San Francisco Giants, July 8, 1970, fifth inning.

SOURCE: *Baseball Digest*

12 Players Who Hit Fewer Than 15 Homers, Yet Drove in 100 or More Runs (Since 1946)

Player, Team	Year	HR	RBI
1. Dixie Walker, Brooklyn	1946	9	116
2. Hoot Evers, Detroit	1948	10	103
3. Enos Slaughter, St. Louis (NL)	1950	10	101
4. Wes Parker, Los Angeles (NL)	1970	10	111
5. Willie Montanez, San Francisco	1975	10	101
6. Enos Slaughter, St. Louis (NL)	1952	11	101
7. Floyd Robinson, Chicago (AL)	1962	11	109
8. Keith Hernandez, St. Louis (NL)	1979	11	105
9. Hank Majeski, Philadelphia (AL)	1948	12	120
10. Ray Jablonski, St. Louis (NL)	1954	12	104
11. Minnie Minoso, Chicago (AL)	1957	12	103
12. Thurman Munson, New York (AL)	1975	12	102

SOURCE: *Baseball Digest*

16 Players Who Had More RBIs Than Games Played (Through 1982)

Player	Year
1. Babe Ruth	1921, 1927, 1929, 1930, 1931, 1932
2. Lou Gehrig	1927, 1930, 1931, 1934, 1937
3. Jimmie Foxx	1930, 1932, 1933, 1938
4. Joe DiMaggio	1937, 1939, 1940, 1948
5. Al Simmons	1927, 1929, 1930

  6. Hank Greenberg 1935, 1937, 1940
  7. Ken Williams   1922, 1925
  8. Hack Wilson   1929, 1930
  9. Rogers Hornsby 1925
 10. Mel Ott   1929
 11. Chuck Klein   1930
 12. Hal Trosky   1936
 13. Vern Stephens   1949
 14. Ted Williams   1949
 15. Walt Dropo   1950
 16. George Brett   1980

SOURCE: National Baseball Hall of Fame and Museum

Baseball's Only All-Switch-Hitting Infield
(Los Angeles Dodgers, 1965)

1b—Wes Parker
2b—Jim Lefebvre
ss—Maury Wills
3b—Jim Gilliam

Baseball's Only All-Lefthanded-Hitting Infield
(Washington Senators, 1937)

1b—Joe Kuhel
2b—Buddy Myer
ss—Cecil Travis
3b—Buddy Lewis

The 7 Best Righthanded Hitters Who Threw Left

	Player	Lifetime Average
1.	Jimmy Ryan	.310
2.	Rube Bressler	.302
3.	Patsy Donovan	.301
4.	Rickey Henderson	.291*

*Through 1982

Though overshadowed by the Babe, Lou Gehrig was a prodigious hitter and a hallmark of the Yankees.

UPI

5. Hal Chase		.291
6. Johnny Cooney		.286
7. Cleon Jones		.280

SOURCE: L. Robert Davids, SABR

45 Players Who Had 100 Walks and 100 Strikeouts in the Same Season

Player, Team	Year	Walks	Strikeouts
1. Jimmie Foxx, Boston (AL)	1936	105	119
2. Hank Greenberg, Detroit	1937	102	101
3. Dolph Camilli, Brooklyn	1938	119	101
4. Dolph Camilli, Brooklyn	1939	110	107
5. Dolph Camilli, Brooklyn	1941	104	115
6. Charlie Keller, New York (AL)	1946	113	101
7. Eddie Joost, Philadelphia (AL)	1947	114	110
8. Mickey Mantle, New York (AL)	1954	102	107
9. Larry Doby, Chicago (AL)	1956	102	105
10. Mickey Mantle, New York (AL)	1958	129	120
11. Mickey Mantle, New York (AL)	1960	111	125
12. Eddie Mathews, Milwaukee (NL)	1960	111	113
13. Bob Allison, Minnesota	1961	103	100
14. Harmon Killebrew, Minnesota	1961	107	109
15. Mickey Mantle, New York (AL)	1961	126	112
16. Harmon Killebrew, Minnesota	1962	106	142
17. Eddie Mathews, Milwaukee (NL)	1963	124	119
18. Harmon Killebrew, Minnesota	1967	131	111
19. Mickey Mantle, New York (AL)	1967	107	113
20. Dick McAuliffe, Detroit	1967	105	118
21. Reggie Jackson, Oakland	1969	114	142
22. Jimmy Wynn, Houston	1969	148	142
23. Dick Dietz, San Francisco	1970	109	106
24. Frank Howard, Washington	1970	132	125
25. Willie Mays, San Francisco	1971	112	123
26. Darrell Evans, Atlanta	1973	124	104
27. Bob Bailey, Montreal	1974	100	107
28. Jimmy Wynn, Los Angeles	1974	108	104
29. Gene Tenace, Oakland	1974	110	105
30. Mike Schmidt, Philadelphia	1974	106	138
31. Darrell Evans, Atlanta	1975	105	106

32. Mike Schmidt, Philadelphia	1975	101	180
33. Gene Tenace, Oakland	1975	106	127
34. Mike Schmidt, Philadelphia	1976	100	149
35. Jimmy Wynn, Atlanta	1976	127	111
36. Mike Schmidt, Philadelphia	1977	104	122
37. Ken Singleton, Baltimore	1977	107	101
38. Gene Tenace, San Diego	1977	125	119
39. Greg Luzinski, Philadelphia	1978	100	135
40. Mike Schmidt, Philadelphia	1979	129	115
41. Ken Singleton, Baltimore	1979	109	118
42. Gene Tenace, San Diego	1979	105	106
43. Mike Schmidt, Philadelphia	1982	107	131
44. Jason Thompson, Pittsburgh	1982	101	107
45. Dwight Evans, Boston	1982	112	125

Submitted by Robert J. Lazzari, SABR

All-Time Team with Highest Single-Season Batting Averages at Each Position (Through 1982)

American League

1b—George Sisler, 1922 (.420)
2b—Napoleon Lajoie, 1901 (.422)
3b—George Brett, 1980 (.390)
ss—Luke Appling, 1936 (.388)
of—Ty Cobb, 1911 (.420)
c—Bill Dickey, 1936 (.362)
p—Walter Johnson, 1925 (.433)

National League

1b—Bill Terry, 1930 (.401)
2b—Rogers Hornsby, 1924 (.424)
3b—Fred Lindstrom, 1930 (.379)
ss—Arky Vaughan, 1935 (.385)
of—Lefty O'Doul, 1929 (.398)
c—Chief Meyers, 1912 (.358)
p—Jack Bentley, 1923 (.427)

SOURCE: National Baseball Hall of Fame and Museum

53 Players with Career Batting Averages under .220 for a Minimum of 1,000 At-Bats (Through 1982)

		At bats	Average
1.	Bill Bergen	3028	.170
2.	Ray Oyler	1265	.175
3.	Fritz Buelow	1299	.189
4.	Mike Ryan	1920	.193
5.	Rich Morales	1053	.195
6.	Sam Agnew	1537	.204
7.	Billy Sullivan	3345	.207
8.	John Henry	1920	.207
9.	Jackie Hernandez	1480	.208
10.	Gabby Street	1501	.208
11.	Luke Boone	1028	.209
12.	Tom Needham	1491	.209
13.	Luis Gomez	1251	.210
14.	Jack Heidemann	1093	.211
15.	Terry Humphrey	1055	.211
16.	Dave Nicholson	1419	.212
17.	Mike Powers	1782	.212
18.	Rusty Torres	1314	.212
19.	Dave Campbell	1252	.213
20.	Jerry Kindall	2057	.213
21.	Red Kleinow	1665	.213
22.	Harry Smith	1004	.213
23.	Dick Tracewski	1231	.213
24.	Mick Kelleher	1081	.213
25.	Luis Alvarado	1160	.214
26.	Lena Blackburne	1807	.214
27.	Dave Duncan	2885	.214
28.	Jeff Torborg	1391	.214
29.	Phil Roof	2151	.215
30.	Bobby Wine	3172	.215
31.	Mario Mendoza	1337	.215
32.	Ray Berres	1330	.216
33.	Hunter Hill	1200	.216
34.	Hector Torres	1738	.216
35.	Steve Swisher	1414	.216

36.	Fred Stanley	1650	.216
37.	Walter Blair	1255	.217
38.	Vic Harris	1610	.217
39.	Ted Kazanski	1329	.217
40.	Clyde Manion	1153	.217
41.	Dal Maxvill	3443	.217
42.	Wes Westrum	2322	.217
43.	Doc White	1279	.217
44.	George McBride	5526	.218
45.	Fred Raymer	1380	.218
46.	John Boccabella	1462	.219
47.	Harry Howell	1263	.219
48.	Billy Hunter	1875	.219
49.	Mike Kahoe	1088	.219
50.	Lou Ritter	1437	.219
51.	Jimmy Smith	1127	.219
52.	Skeeter Webb	2274	.219
53.	Al Weis	1578	.219

SOURCE: Bob Rosen, Elias Sports Bureau, who says: "The list is limited to non-pitchers and only records from 1901 were used. [Editor's note: 1901 begins the modern era of baseball.] If a player appeared prior to 1901, only his figures compiled from 1901 on were used."

Rosen also notes that hitting improved in 1930 and began to decline in the '60s. It should also be pointed out that the 53 men listed obviously had some skill to have stayed in the major leagues long enough to acquire 1,000 at-bats. Many were defensive specialists; catchers and shortstops, in particular, dominate the list.

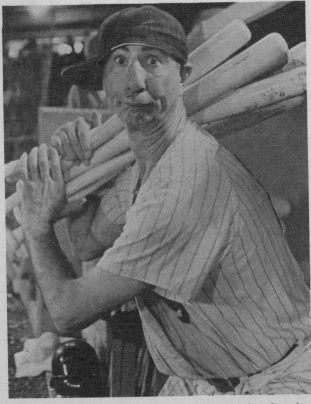

He never landed in the box score, but Max Patkin made it to the majors as a clown.

Max Patkin Collection

IV

The Human Comedy

Max Patkin's 9 Favorite Clowns

Max Patkin is baseball's famous clown and, of course, belongs on the top of any list of clowns. He has taken his 6-3 double-jointed body and rubber face all over the world and entertained millions with his side-splitting antics. It all began during World War II when Patkin, a serious pitcher at the time, pitched to Joe DiMaggio, who promptly belted Max' Sunday pitch off the island of Oahu in the Hawaiians. Patkin threw his glove to the ground, twisted his hat sideways and followed DiMaggio around the bases as thousands roared. Patkin has been clowning ever since, once as a coach for Bill Veeck's Browns for an entire season.

1. Jackie Price—Naturally, my old partner (we teamed up with the Cleveland Indians in 1946) is first on the list. He was part trickster and part comic. His tricks included batting upside-down, catching fly balls while riding in a jeep, etc.
2. Goose Tatum—He was the funniest man who ever performed in a ball park. He traveled with the Harlem

Globetrotters for years and was known as "The Clown Prince of Basketball." He used an oversized first base-man's mitt and played for the Indianapolis Clowns and the Kansas City Monarchs. He had long arms and was funny-looking.

3. Billy Mills—Son of the old Detroit Tiger coach. He currently resides in Utica, NY. He was a funny guy and he performed in the minor leagues in the late '40s and '50s. Did a great imitation of Babe Ruth.

4. The House of David—I'm putting this team down as a unit. They all wore beards and represented a religious order out of Benton Harbor, MI, and traveled around the country in the late '20s, '30s and '40s. They were a very good team and put on pre-game pepper shows and were very funny when they wanted to be. They basically recruited ballplayers who grew beards. Bill Steinecke, who worked for the Atlanta Braves and Montreal Expos and managed several minor league clubs, did a lot of comedy for them.

5. Ed Hannum—He was the only white man who traveled with the Indianapolis Clowns in the '40s, '50s and '60s. He was a funny guy who eventually bought the Clowns' team. But due to sagging attendance and the inability to get good ballparks to play in, he eventually sold the team which folded up a few years ago. In the end, the team was comprised of black and white college kids.

6. Johnny Jones—He traveled the minor league circuit in a car on which he painted the name of every city he appeared in. Did a trick show with bats, exploding bats, and was a great juggler.

7. Wes Shulmerick—Was stationed in Kanahoe, Hawaii, with a Navy team and managed the club in 1944. Among his players were Johnny Mize, Sherry Robertson, Tom Ferrick. He was a funny, funny guy.

8. Chesty (Chet) Johnson—Played in the Pacific Coast League for years in the '40s and '50s. He wasn't a funny-looking guy, but he had many funny things he did while he pitched. He would take out a book and begin reading while on the mound, and he would use powder puffs under his arms, etc.

9. Billy Shuster—A very funny fellow who played short-stop in the Pacific Coast League in the late '30s, '40s and '50s.

Note: At the risk of overlooking some people, I'll add some names of players who were colorful and funny in their own way. Naturally, Dizzy Dean was colorful and funny; Jim Piersall was quite zany and unpredictable; Jay Johnstone is a flake; Mark (The Bird) Fidrych with his antics on the mound; and Zeke Bonura was just a character, funny-looking and with a big schnozz.

Ernie Harwell's 10 Things Bound To Happen on the Team Bus

Ernie Harwell has been riding the team bus for over 40 years as one of the top baseball broadcasters in the business. For the past 22 years, he has been the voice of the Detroit Tigers.

1. The driver will be fat.
2. Above the dashboard, the driver will have a new league baseball to be autographed by the players.
3. The player who wandered aimlessly off first base and was picked off in last night's game will give the driver directions to the ball park.
4. Before the bus has gone three blocks, at least four players will yell for more air-conditioning.
5. An elderly lady will board the bus at a stop light and ask, "Is this the D bus to Glen Cove?"
6. The team manager will sit in the front of the bus and the loudest stereos will blast from the back.
7. Somebody will have news—or at least a rumor—of a brand-new big league trade.
8. The ugliest man on the team will shout out of his window at a fairly attractive young lady—and tell her how ugly she is.
9. At least one player will be working a crossword puzzle.
10. The worst-dressed passengers will be members of the media.

Ernie Harwell's 10 Things Certain To Happen during a Baseball Rain Delay

1. Everybody will desert the box seat area, but three kids with plastic over their heads will remain there throughout the rain.
2. The organist will play "Raindrops Keep Falling on My Head," "Singing in the Rain," and four other rain songs.
3. A banner in the center field bleachers will become so soaked that all the lettering will run together.
4. A rookie utility infielder will hope for more rain, so he can attend a downtown movie.
5. Three young ladies will run to the box seat section and try to talk with some of the players in the home dugout. The players will ignore them, but the batboy will make points.
6. Four or five players will stay in each dugout. At least one player in each dugout will be fondling a bat.
7. Two sports writers will locate a well-endowed young lady in the stands and train binoculars on her.
8. Another writer will re-visit the press room to devour two more ham and cheese sandwiches.
9. A youngster will dash from the stands onto the field and slide on the tarp.
10. At the height of the downpour some loud-mouth fan will yell, at nobody in particular, "Play Ball!"

Ernie Harwell's 10 Goofiest Baseball Trades

1. Chattanooga shortstop Johnny Jones was traded to Charlotte, N.C., for a Thanksgiving turkey.
2. Canton, Ohio, peddled the great Cy Young to Cleveland for a suit of clothes.
3. The Red Sox sent Babe Ruth to the Yankees for a mortgage on Fenway Park.
4. The Detroit Tigers paid the spring training rent to Augusta, Ga., by leaving Ed Cicotte with the Augusta team.

5. Lefty Grove moved from Martinsburg, W. Va., to Baltimore in exchange for a center field fence.
6. Dallas sent pitcher Joe Martina to New Orleans in exchange for two barrels of oysters.
7. First baseman Jack Fenton went from San Francisco to the Memphis team for a box of prunes.
8. Nashville's Larry Gilbert gave up a set of golf clubs to obtain catcher Greek George.
9. In 1944, as part-owner and pitcher for Little Rock, Willis Hudlin sold himself to the St. Louis Browns. After the Browns had won the pennant and Hudlin had received a World Series share, owner Hudlin repurchased pitcher Hudlin for a cheaper price and kept the change.
10. Montreal catcher Cliff Dapper was traded to the Atlanta Crackers for baseball announcer Ernie Harwell.

Irving Rudd's 4 Greatest Brooklyn Dodger Fans

Long ago, in a never-never land called Brooklyn, there was a baseball team named the Dodgers. It came to pass that baseball was synonymous with Brooklyn and Brooklyn was synonymous with Dodgers and they had the wackiest, craziest, most wonderful fans in all of sports. Irving Rudd remembers the Dodgers, their fans and Ebbets Field well. He was promotion director for the Brooklyn Dodgers from 1951 through 1957, after which the Dodgers left Brooklyn. Baseball, Brooklyn and Irving Rudd have never been the same. He's currently director of publicity for Top Rank, Inc.

1. The Dodger Sym-phony band: Actually comprised of five members, but thought of as one. Brother Lou Soriano, horn; Jerry Martin, snare drum; Jo Jo Delio, cymbals; Paddy Palma, bass drum; Phil Cacavalle, trumpet. They would parade through the stands "entertaining" fans with something that closely resembled music.
2 Hilda Chester: Queen of the Cowbell. This huge woman was a loyal Dodger fan who rarely missed a game. She

The Brooklyn Dodgers' Sym-phony band serenades club president Walter O'Malley in 1951.

UPI

would sit in her seat and cheer for her heroes in a shrill voice abetted by her cowbell, which she would clang at the appropriate time.

3. Eddie Bettan: From the 1920s on, he carried a shrill whistle. He would pick out a particular Dodger player and whistle at him.

4. Fierce Jack Pierce: He had a thing for Cookie Lavagetto. Sat in a box seat right near the Dodger dugout and would scream, "Cook-ee, Cook-ee, Cook-ee." Carried an air machine that could blow up balloons. Every time Lavagetto came to bat, Fierce Jack Pierce would blow up a balloon and float it into the air.

Irving Rudd's 6 Top Promotion Stunts at Ebbets Field

1. Musical Depreciation Night: With the Dodger Sym-phony Band as catalyst, Rudd, in association with Dodger president Walter O'Malley, gave free admission to the ballpark to any fan with a musical instrument, kazoos and tissue paper combs included. Two guys rolled a piano across the rotunda. This was the Dodger response to officials of musicians union local 802, who demanded that the Sym-phony be paid for its appearances. The union backed off the next day.

2. Camera Day: Still being used by the Dodgers in Los Angeles.

3. General Douglas MacArthur Day: The General appeared at Ebbets Field in 1951, shortly after he was relieved of his command by President Truman. He loved seeing the Dodgers play. He attended 13 games. The Dodgers never won when he came. That's the year they blew the 13½-game lead to the Giants.

4. PeeWee Reese Night: In honor of the Dodgers' captain on his 36th birthday. Capacity crowd. It was the first time that the fans were not permitted to contribute their hard-earned money. The business community was solicited for gifts. The result: a brand new Chevrolet, clothes, vacation trips, sporting gear, golf clubs, etc., more than $10,000 in gifts, and this was 1955. A 250-pound birthday cake was lit while the ballpark was

darkened and the crowd, holding candles or matches, sang "Happy Birthday."

5. Jersey City Ticket Sales: As the one-eleventh business manager of the Brooklyn Dodgers (seven home games out of 77 were played in Jersey City), Rudd sold the first two tickets of the season to a 12-year-old grammar school student named Willie Mays and a high school student named Bill Rigney. Another Bill Rigney was the Giants' manager that season.

6. The Dog Who Stopped The Game: A mongrel dog loped onto the field near third base. First PeeWee Reese, then Billy Cox, then the grounds crew tried to grab him. The dog held up the game for more than 15 minutes. Rudd says he had absolutely nothing to do with the dog, it was purely accidental. "To this day I get credit for the 'stunt,' " Rudd says sheepishly.

12 Well-Known, or Infamous, Tobacco Chewers

1. Danny Murtaugh—He delighted in picking out sports writers wearing white shoes and spraying the shoes with juice.

2. Ralph Houk—His thing was to sneak up behind unsuspecting, preoccupied players, and shoot a squirt in their back pocket.

3. Steve Hamilton—One fateful day in Kansas City, while pitching for the Yankees, he swallowed his chaw and threw up all over the pitcher's mound.

4. Catfish Hunter—"I started chewing in high school. My coach wouldn't let us chew bubble gum ever since a guy on first base blew a bubble and missed the steal sign. I chewed all the time, even at home, but never when I was pitching because I was afraid of swallowing the thing."

5. Tobacco Johnny Lanning—His nickname tells it all.

6. Nellie Fox—"I always thought he had the mumps," says Yogi Berra, an occasional chewer.

7. Harvey Kuenn—"I believe he chewed when he slept," says Al Rosen.

8. Sparky Lyle

9. Rocky Bridges

10. Johnny Sain
11. Don Zimmer
12. Rod Carew

7 Well-Known Cigar Smokers in Baseball

1. Jimmy Dykes—Became immortalized as a cigar smoker when, as a player, he failed to slide into third. "I couldn't," he explained. "I carry my cigars in my back pocket and I was afraid I'd break them."
2. Ralph Houk—Switches from cigars to chewing tobacco once a game starts and back again without hardly missing a beat.
3. Luis Tiant—Cuban cigars, of course.
4. Babe Ruth—Smoked cigars as he did everything else, to excess.
5. Branch Rickey—Churchillian in demeanor, eloquence, and always-present cigar, which he used to punctuate his oratory.
6. Joe Torre—The humidor on his desk in the Braves' clubhouse is always well-stocked.
7. Johnny Mize—Put his cigar down long enough to hit 359 career homers, 51 for the New York Giants in 1947.

Morganna's 10 Favorite Players "I Would Most Like to Run Out on the Field and Kiss"

Known as "Baseball's Kissing Bandit," exotic dancer Morganna has been sneaking out onto baseball fields all over the country to plant a kiss on unsuspecting ballplayers. There have been no formal complaints filed, either from players or fans, who enjoy watching Morganna sprint to paydirt in sneakers, shorts and a tight-fitting sweater.

Pete Rose was the first player smooched by Morganna back in 1969, when she started her act. Since then, she has popped onto the field 12 times and got her man on all but two occasions.

Alas, there was never a championship cigar for Joe Torre when he managed the Mets.

"Pretty good batting average, huh!" she points out.

Morganna has no intention of retiring. She nailed George Brett at the 1980 All-Star Game and he immediately went to the top of her list.

1. George Brett—He's a great kisser and a fantastic baseball player.
2. Jim Palmer—He looks so cute in his undies.
3. Rick Cerone—I'm from the South and my grandmother told me never to kiss a Yankee, but for him I'll make an exception.
4. Pete Rose—He's always been my baseball idol.
5. Steve Carlton—I've always liked the strong, silent type.
6. Nolan Ryan
7. Tom Seaver
8. Fred Lynn
9. Bucky Dent
10. (tie) Joe Garagiola—My favorite baseball announcer.
    San Diego Chicken—My favorite chicken.
    Billy Martin—My favorite manager.

Gabe Paul's 9 Observations Culled from a Half Century in Baseball

Gabe Paul, who started in the game as a batboy in Rochester, N.Y., has done it all in more than 50 years in baseball. Currently, he is President of the Cleveland Indians.

1. Favorite Book—*The Long Season,* by Jim Brosnan.
2. Strangest Baseball Scene—Grover Cleveland Alexander going into an epileptic seizure and throwing a third strike to Don Hurst.
3. A Memorable Incident—George Stallings telling a rookie who wondered what smelled: "It's my breath you so-and-so, but you won't be here long enough to smell it."
4. An Unforgettable Incident—When a train developed a "hot box," Steve Bilko disembarked and when they blew the whistle to re-board Steve came running down the track with a case of beer on his shoulder.

5. Greatest Waste of Talent—Joe Taylor, once with the A's. Booze. Wrecked three cars in one night.
6. Biggest Eater (Meat and Potatoes)—Jim Turner.
7. Most Eccentric Sportswriter—Jack Ryder, Cincinnati, who ate hard boiled eggs, shells and all, and cheese triangles, tinfoil and all.
8. Greatest Baseball Mind—Branch Rickey.
9. Most Colorful and Memorable Commissioner—Judge Landis.

Mickey Lolich's 4 Favorite Pastries

Mickey Lolich, eighth on the all-time strikeout list going into the 1983 season, was almost as famous for his protruding potbelly as he was for his pitching prowess with the Detroit Tigers. Lolich now owns and operates a doughnut and pastry shop in Rochester, Mich., but insists he only eats "a couple of doughnuts a day." He says his weight is 222, just four pounds over his pitching weight.

1. Chocolate-covered fry cakes
2. Cinnamon twists
3. Apple fritters
4. French crullers

Submitted by Jim Hawkins, author of Ron LeFlore's autobiography, *Breakout*, and a former baseball writer for the Detroit *Free Press*. He is now a Detroit-based free-lance writer, among other things.

Arnold C. Brackman's 9 Best Places from Which to Listen to a Baseball Game

Arnold C. (Brack) Brackman, ex-foreign correspondent and author, likes to listen to the play-by-play on radio. Brackman's last two books were Book-of-the-Month selections—*The Luck of Ninveh: Archeology's Great Adventure* and *A Delicate Arrangement: The Strange Case of Charles Darwin and Alfred Russell Wallace*.

1. Submarine—Most announcers are all wet.
2. Zoo—Peanuts are available and if it is a Yankee game, that's the only place.
3. Wall Street—So you can empathize with the players' problems.
4. Trout Stream—Listening to announcers, you need hip boots.
5. Coal Mine—Announcers usually keep you in the dark, anyway.
6. Circus—Which is what the grand old game has settled into, with agents, accountants, lawyers, labor arbiters, etc.
7. Niagara Falls—To drown out the bullspit.
8. Pyramid—The crowd's roar reverberates better.
9. Home—As in baseball, there is nothing like heading home.

Frank Boggs' 10 Favorite Things About Baseball

1. Home run in the bottom of the ninth
2. Hot hot dog
3. Cold beer
4. Cold hot dog
5. Fairly cold beer
6. Seeing visiting manager thumbed
7. Luke-warm beer
8. Extra innings
9. Really warm beer
10. Rest room

Note: When he isn't watching baseball games and drinking beer, Frank Boggs writes sports for the Colorado Springs *Sun*.

Don Stanhouse's Top 5 Baseball Flakes

Dubbed "Stan The Man Unusual" by Oriole teammate Mike Flanagan, Don Stanhouse knows a flake when he sees one, but he says there is a shortage of flakes in baseball. Modestly, he places himself fifth on his list.

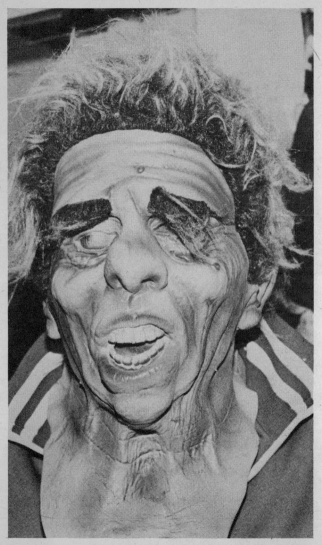

The Dodgers' Jay Johnstone wears his horror mask as the team celebrates a World Series triumph over the Yankees in 1981.

UPI

1. Jay Johnstone
2. Joe Pepitone
3. Dave Goltz
4. Jerry Reuss
5. Don Stanhouse

Note: Stanhouse lists Steve Garvey as "a closet sickie. You'd be surprised what some of these All-American type guys do." About Goltz, Stanhouse adds: "He's a real normal guy. He'll put the cat out every day at 6 p.m., never 6:01. But get him together with Reuss and. . . ."

Red Foley's Recollections of 7 of 72 Who Played Third Base in New York Mets' History

As a staffer for the New York *Daily News* and a follower of the Mets since Day One, Red Foley has kept track of the enormous traffic at third base in Shea Stadium. He counted 72 in the team's history at the mid-point of the 1982 season and he has selected seven that bring a chuckle.

1. Don Zimmer—Of the 72 guys who have played one or more games at third for the Mets, Don Zimmer was the first. Zim got hits in each of the club's first three games, then went on an 0-for-34 "tear." He broke it with a hit on May 4 in Philly and two days later, after going four-for-52 (.076) for the Mets, was dealt to the Reds.
2. Cliff Cook—He was part of Cincinnati's contribution to the deal for Zimmer and he was supposed to be a third baseman. Cook's Met career was 16 games in that 1962 season, as a third baseman, and it quickly became apparent he couldn't play because he couldn't bend with his bad back.
3. Felix Mantilla—The Mets played nine different men at third in 1962 and Mantilla, with 95 appearances, led the lot in that regard. Felix, who two years later hit 30 homers playing for the Red Sox at Fenway Park, only made 14 errors in 269 chances at third for the Mets in '62, but most remember him as a third baseman who invariably broke to his right on ground balls to his left

and vice versa. A lot of potential ground outs became base hits as a result.

4. Rich Herrscher—Late in their first season, the Mets imported Rick Herrscher and his Mets' career lasted six games at third base. That he didn't hit his weight and was charged with two errors in 12 chances wasn't as bad for him as the performance he put on in front of the Mets' dugout during a pre-game Chubby Checker concert. The rock 'n roll was blasting everyone's ears and, suddenly, there's Herrscher doing the twist with some broad from the show. Casey Stengel, in the dugout, took one look, screwed up his face like a vise and you knew Herrscher wasn't long for the Metsies. He wasn't.

5. Charlie Neal—When the 1963 season opened, the Mets' front office was proclaiming vast improvement over the team that lost 120 games in its first year. The St. Louis Cardinals provided the opposition on opening day and Roger Craig's first pitch was tapped to third baseman Charlie Neal. He picked up the ball and overthrew the first baseman to touch off St. Louis' 7-0 victory. After the game, manager Casey Stengel opened his post-game press conference by snarling, ''We're still frauds—we cheated the attendance again.''

6. Joe Moock—Another interesting debut was that of Joe Moock, up from the minors in 1967, on the weekend of Sept. 2-3 in Chicago. Moock was inserted in the Sunday game around the seventh inning by manager Wes Westrum and Moock, who was to make three errors in 36 chances in his 12-game Mets' career, did it ala Neal and heaved the ball over the first baseman's head.

7. Jim Fregosi—In 1972, after he had been acquired from the Angels in the Nolan Ryan deal that winter, Jim Fregosi joined the Mets. He had been an all-star shortstop in the '60s with California, but Fregosi, who hadn't played at third in his 11 seasons with the Angels, was proclaimed the Mets' third sacker. The Mets' people all said he'd have no trouble making the switch, but in the first exhibition game, at Sarasota against the White Sox, he missed the first ground ball hit to him. The next day, at Bradenton, while taking pre-game grounders hit by manager Gil Hodges, Fregosi suffered a broken finger and though he played third for the Mets most of that season, Diamond Jim made no one forget Brooks Robinson.

Jim Fregosi left his glove in California when he joined the Mets.

UPI

Master of the slide and the stolen base, Lou Brock takes a busman's holiday with his family.

UPI

V

A Level of Greatness

Maury Will's 10 Greatest Base Stealers

When it comes to stealing bases, Maury Wills knows his business. The Dodger swifty was the first man in baseball history to steal more than 100 bases in a single season and his 104 steals in 1962 broke a record (Ty Cobb's 96) that had stood for 47 years. Wills was something of a trend-setter. Since he began terrorizing pitchers on the basepaths, the stolen base has become a more prevalent weapon in the game. His record stood for only 12 seasons and was broken by Lou Brock, who swiped 118 bases in 1974.

Wills' list is restricted to players he saw.

1. Lou Brock
2. Davey Lopes
3. Luis Aparicio
4. Rickey Henderson
5. Willie Wilson
6. Tim Raines

7. Joe Morgan
8. Omar Moreno
9. Bobby Bonds
10. Ron LeFlore

8 Best Base-Stealing Tandems of All Time

1. Ron LeFlore (96) and Rodney Scott (63), Montreal, 1980 159
2. Rickey Henderson (130) and Dwayne Murphy (26), Oakland, 1982 156
3. Lou Brock, (118) and Bake McBride (30), St. Louis, NL, 1974 148
4. Clyde Milan (75) and Danny Moeller (62), Washington, 1913 137
5. Maury Wills (104) and Willie Davis (32), Los Angeles, 1962 136
6. Ty Cobb (96) and Donie Bush (35), Detroit, 1915 131
7. Ty Cobb (76) and Donie Bush (53), Detroit, 1909 129
8. Bill North (75) and Bert Campaneris (54), Oakland, 1976 129

15 Outstanding Players Who Never Played in a World Series

1. George Sisler
2. Ernie Banks
3. Luke Appling
4. Ted Lyons
5. Billy Williams
6. Ralph Kiner
7. Addie Joss
8. Napoleon Lajoie
9. Rod Carew
10. Phil Niekro
11. Gaylord Perry

12. Jim Bunning
13. Ferguson Jenkins
14. Lindy McDaniel
15. Bobby Bonds

15 Momentous National League Happenings in the Month of June

1. June 4, 1968—Don Drysdale of the Dodgers blanked the Pirates for his sixth straight shutout en route to a record 58⅔ scoreless innings.
2. June 10, 1944—Joe Nuxhall, 15 years and 10 months, became the youngest player ever to appear in a major league game when he pitched two-thirds of an inning for the Cincinnati Reds in an 18-0 defeat by the Cardinals.
3. June 11, 1967—The Chicago Cubs hit seven home runs and the New York Mets hit four to tie a major league record set by the Yankees (six) and Tigers (five) in 1950.
4. June 12, 1980—John Richmond of Worcester pitched the first perfect game in history, shutting out Cleveland, 1-0.
5. June 15, 1938—Johnny Vander Meer of the Cincinnati Reds pitched his second straight no-hit game, defeating the Dodgers, 6-0, in the first night game played in Brooklyn.
6. June 16, 1978—Tom Seaver of the Cincinnati Reds pitched his first no-hitter against the Cardinals.
7. June 17, 1915—George (Zip) Zabel of the Cubs was called into the game against Brooklyn with two out in the first. He won, 4-3, in the 19th, the longest relief effort in major league history.
8. June 19, 1973—Pete Rose of the Reds and Willie Davis of the Dodgers both collected career hit No. 2,000.
9. June 21, 1964—Jim Bunning pitched a perfect game for the Phillies over the Mets, giving him a no-hitter in each league.
10. June 22, 1982—Pete Rose of the Phillies moved into second place on the career hit list when he doubled in a game against the Cardinals for hit No. 3,772 (Ty Cobb has the major league mark of 4,191).

Joe Nuxhall was 15 when he pitched for the Cincinnati Reds in 1944.
UPI

11. June 22, 1976—Randy Jones of the Padres tied the 63-year old record of Christy Mathewson by pitching his 68th consecutive inning without allowing a walk.

12. June 23, 1973—Ken Brett of the Phillies hit a home run in the fourth consecutive game that he pitched in June.

13. June 28, 1971—Rick Wise of the Phillies pitched a no-hitter over the Reds and also hit two home runs in the 4-0 victory.

14. June 29, 1897—Chicago scored in every inning and set a major league record for runs as the Cubs defeated Louisville, 36-7.

15. June 30, 1978—Willie McCovey of the Giants hit his 500th career home run in Atlanta, the 12th major leaguer to reach that plateau.

Joe DiMaggio's 4 Greatest Highlights of His Career

Approaching his 70th birthday—the occasion will be marked on November 25, 1984—Joe DiMaggio, named baseball's greatest living player in a recent poll, is more famous than ever because of his television commercials. He seems to grow in stature and dignity with each passing year. Recently, DiMaggio was asked to select his all-time Yankee team and his all-opponent team. "I'd rather not get into that," he said. "I'd leave off somebody who deserves to be on." However, he did admit that any all-opponent team would have to include two men—"My hitter would be Ted Williams and my pitcher would be Bobby Feller"—and he did agree to list the four highlights of his illustrious career.

1. Playing on 10 American League championship teams and 9 World Championship teams in 13 seasons: "That was the most outstanding thing about my career, the highlight, playing with so many world champions; playing with so many great guys through the years. One of my biggest thrills was reporting to spring training in St. Petersburg for the first time in 1936. I had driven from San Francisco with Tony Lazzeri and Frank Crosetti. It took five days. I walked into this dingy

clubhouse that had spikes to hang our clothes, and I
looked around and there was Bill Dickey, Charley
Ruffing, Lou Gehrig, all these great players I had read
about, and it was a thrill to meet these fellows.''

2. Hitting in 56 consecutive games in 1941: ''The Yankees had packed the park day after day because of the
streak, everybody anticipating the record. After the
season, I went to Ed Barrow (Yankee general manager)
and asked for more money. He said it was going to be
difficult to give me more because he didn't know where
we were going—World War II had just broken out. He
offered me a contract with a $5,000 cut. I walked out
of his office without signing and went to my apartment
on Riverside Drive. When I got there, Mark Roth, our
traveling secretary, was waiting for me. He had beat
me home and he was waiting with a contract that called
for the same money as the 1941 season, $37,500.
That's what got out in the newspapers. There was no
mention of the $5,000 they wanted to cut me. It also
got out that I was asking for a $5,000 raise, and I got
tons of mail denouncing me. 'My boy is in the service
making $21 a month and you're asking $42,500.' ''

3. Coming back in Boston after missing the first 65 games
of the 1949 season because of the removal of a bone
spur on his right heel, and hitting four home runs and
driving in nine runs in a three-game series: ''For four
days before the Boston series, I took batting practice in
New York with Gus Niarhos catching and Al Schacht,
60 years old at the time, pitching. Nobody knew when
I was going to play. When reporters asked Casey Stengel
when I was going to play, Casey said, 'When Joe feels
he's ready to come back, I will put him in the lineup.'

''But I knew when I was going to play. I wasn't
going to give that Boston ballpark up. We were only
going to play there one more time that year. What
better place to come back?

''On the day of the first game of the Series, I flew up
to Boston. I didn't go to the hotel. I went straight to the
ballpark, got into my uniform, and went out to the
dugout. Stengel was sitting there with his back to me,
talking to reporters. They were all asking for the starting lineup. 'I can't give you the lineup yet,' Casey said,
and he kept looking at me as I was tying my shoe. He

kept looking and looking and I never said a word. Finally, I nodded my head. And Casey said, 'Now I can give you the lineup.'

"The first time up, I just couldn't seem to get around on the ball. Mickey McDermott was pitching, and he could throw hard and my timing was off. I kept fouling pitches off to right field, but each time I fouled one off, I got around on the ball a little more. Finally, I hit it over the shortstop's head for a single. The next time up, I hit one out of the park. And that started it. And believe me, what I did in those three games was more surprising to me than anybody else."

4. Winning Game No. 2 of the 1950 World Series with a home run in the 10th inning off Robin Roberts of the Philadelphia Phillies: "Up to that time, I hadn't had a hit in the Series. The Phillies started Jim Konstanty in the first game, a surprise because he was a relief pitcher. He pitched a great game, but we won, 1-0. But Konstanty held me hitless.

"When I came to bat in the 10th inning of the second game against Roberts, I was still hitless—going nothing for seven or eight in the Series. The score was tied, 1-1. I remember Bugs Baer wrote that I was hitting up a smokestack, and that's what I was doing.

"Before the game, I asked John Mize what Roberts threw, because he had hit against him in the National League. He said he threw a fastball and a curve. I asked him what Roberts' fastball did and he said it bore in on you. So I tried to open up on him so I wouldn't get jammed, but his fastball kept tailing away from me, not bearing in, and I kept popping him up. I decided to use my own judgment and to concentrate a little harder, and in the 10th inning, I hit one out of the park and we won the game, 2-1."

Phil Rizzuto's 4 Best Bunters of All Time

As a player, Phil Rizzuto used the bunt artfully to enhance his offensive skills. The radio and television "Voice of the Yankees" for 25 years, Rizzuto was hired by owner George Steinbrenner as spring training bunting coach with the hope of returning the art of bunting to the Yankees.

Philadelphia's Pete Rose eyes Ty Cobb's major league hit record.
Nancy Hogue

Rizzuto has decried the bunt as a dying art and insists, "The bunt is one of the easiest things in baseball to learn. All it takes is a delicate touch and a little practice."

1. Phil Rizzuto—Would George Steinbrenner hire the second-best bunter?
2. Rod Carew—"When he was winning those batting titles, Carew must have got 30-40 bunt base hits a year."
3. Mickey Mantle—"Nobody was a better drag bunter. He used to be so fast that he could just outrun the ball."
4. Nellie Fox—"He had a good trick when he bunted: he made sure to leave the bat right where the catcher would trip over it."

Commissioner Bowie Kuhn's 10 Greatest Thrills

1. The Miracle Mets of 1969.
2. Brooks Robinson's play in the 1970 World Series.
3. Roberto Clemente's performance in the 1971 World Series.
4. Henry Aaron's 714th and 715th home runs.
5. Lou Brock's stolen base feats—118 in a single season (and, in 1977, 893 for a career, surpassing Ty Cobb's modern record).
6. The 1975 World Series, particularly the sixth game.
7. The "Fidrych Syndrome"—the remarkable interaction between the fans and players, which started to happen frequently in 1976.
8. Reggie Jackson's four consecutive home runs in the 1977 World Series.
9. Pete Rose's 44-game consecutive hitting streak in 1978.
10. The Yankees' comeback in 1978.

Editor's Note: Commissioner Kuhn limited his "thrills" to events that took place on the playing field during his time as commissioner. His choices are listed chronologically and not in order of preference, because "it would be extremely difficult to say which event has been the most pleasing."

Henry Aaron socks No. 715, the home run that beat the Babe's all-time mark.

UPI

Keith Morris' 9 Best Baseball Interviewees

Keith Morris, special events and publicity director for *Sports Illustrated,* is the voice of SI's syndicated radio show that is heard on more than 300 stations.

1. Casey Stengel
2. Ted Williams
3. Joe DiMaggio
4. Pete Rose
5. Pie Traynor
6. Willie Mays
7. Roberto Clemente
8. Hank Aaron
9. Whitey Ford

Leo Durocher's 11 Greatest Umpires

In his half century in baseball, as a player, coach and manager, colorful, controversial, fiery Leo Durocher had his share of arguments with umpires. Still, he respects and recognizes the job umpires do and agreed to submit his list of the greatest umpires of all time.

1. Bill Klem
2. Al Barlick
3. Dolly Stark
4. Tom Gorman
5. Shag Crawford
6. Doug Harvey
7. Bruce Froemming
8. Chris Pelakoudas
9. Ed Vargo
10. Ed Sudol
11. Billy Williams

Durocher adds: "In my opinion, these are the best ones, but it's only my personal opinion. I don't like to rate them,

Casey Stengel: Let me make myself perfectly clear.

but these were the best while I was around. I chose all National Leaguers because I don't know the American League that well.''

11 Greatest Baseball Players from Georgia

1. Ty Cobb
*2. Luke Appling
3. Johnny Mize
4. Spud Chandler
5. Cecil Travis
6. Whitlow Wyatt
7. Jim Hearn
8. Marty Marion
9. Erskine Mayer
10. Nap Rucker
*11. Jackie Robinson

Selected by Furman Bisher of the Atlanta *Journal*

*Jackie Robinson was regarded as more a Californian than a Georgian. And Bisher notes that "Luke Appling is not a native Georgian. He was born in North Carolina, but lived there a shorter time than Robinson's two years in Georgia."

Keith Olbermann's 10 Greatest World Series Games

1. Game 6, 1975—The image of Carlton Fisk, standing at home plate, urging his 12th-inning, game-winning home run off Pat Darcy into fair territory, is etched in the minds of millions of fans, but it was only the capper. The Sox had gone ahead early on a three-run homer from Fred Lynn, only to see the Reds surge to a 6-3 lead. Then Bernie Carbo's second pinch-hit homer of the Series tied it in the eighth, setting up a bases-loaded, none-out situation in the 10th. The Red Sox failed to capitalize on it, making Fisk's homer that much more dramatic.
2. Game 4, 1947—For two hours Ebbets Field agonized with Yankee pitcher Floyd (Bill) Bevens as this histor-

Johnny Mize was The Big Cat out of Demorest, Georgia, a slugging first baseman who spent 15 years in the bigs with the Cardinals, the Giants and the Yankees.

UPI

ically mediocre pitcher flirted with the Series' first no-hitter. Bevens' wildness—with two out in the ninth he had walked nine—had given the Dodgers a run without a hit as the Yankees led, 2-1. With a runner on second and two out in the ninth, Yankee manager Bucky Harris ordered the winning run intentionally walked. The pinch-hitter, Cookie Lavagetto, lined a shot off the right field fence to drive in the tying and winning runs. Ironically, it was the last big league game for both Bevens and Lavagetto.

3. Game 7, 1960—Like the sixth game of 1975, this one was reduced to one hit, the game and series-deciding homer by Bill Mazeroski. Earlier there had been two stunning plays—the tailor-made double play ball that hit a pebble and hit Yankee shortstop Tony Kubek in the Adam's Apple, opening the gates for a five-run eighth-inning rally, highlighted by a three-run homer from back-up Pirate catcher Hal Smith. Almost forgotten, too, is the Yankees' two-run rally in the ninth that made Maz' homer possible and necessary and giving the Pirates the World Series victory in what would be Casey Stengel's last game as Yankee manager.

4. Game 8, 1912—History has condensed, in this case unfairly, a magnificent game into a one-play affair, "The Fred Snodgrass Error." The game was more than that one play, a great pitching duel between the Giants' Christy Mathewson and Boston's Hugh Bedient and Smokey Joe Wood, then a thrilling extra-inning contest. The Giants led, 2-1, in the bottom of the 10th when center fielder Snodgrass dropped pinch-hitter Clyde Engle's fly for a two-base error. On the next play, Snodgrass made a tremendous catch on Harry Hooper's fly and nearly doubled Engle at second. Mathewson then walked Steve Yerkes and helped cause the crucial error of the series, dropping Tris Speaker's foul pop after a mixup with catcher Chief Meyers and first baseman Fred Merkle. Speaker then singled Engle home and moments later Yerkes scored the winning run on a sacrifice fly.

5. Game 4, 1929—The Cubs led the A's, 8-0, in the bottom of the seventh, then all hell broke loose. The A's scored 10 runs off Charlie Root and two Cub relievers. The Cubs still led, 8-3, when Mule Haas

Bill Mazeroski nears the plate as fans and Pirate coach Frank Oceak (44) surround him after World Series-winning clout against the Yankees in 1960.

UPI

flied to center where Hack Wilson lost the ball in the blinding sun and it rocketed past him for an inside-the-park, three-run homer.

6. Game 5, 1956—This was the game in which the Yankees' Don Larsen rather routinely set down 27 consecutive Dodger batters for the Series' only perfect game. Larsen used only 97 pitches, the last an uncertain called third strike past pinch-hitter Dale Mitchell. Brooklyn's Sal Maglie allowed just two runs and five hits.

7. Game 7, 1926—Only one moment of this game was truly great. The Cards led, 3-2, in the seventh when the Yankees loaded the bases with two out. Called in to relieve starter Jesse Haines was 39-year-old Grover Cleveland Alexander, who had pitched a complete-game victory the day before. Alex, although possibly hung over, pushed a called strike past the dangerous Tony Lazzeri, got Lazzeri to hit foul for strike two, then fanned him on the third pitch to put down the rally. Alex then breezed through the next two innings to nail down the game and the Series.

8. Game 5, 1920—This bizarre game, won by the Indians, 8-1, saw the losing Dodgers outhit the Tribe, 13-12. But Cleveland second baseman Bill Wambsganss helped make up the difference with the only unassisted triple play in World Series history. The game also featured the Series' first grand slam, by Cleveland's Elmer Smith, the first homer by a pitcher (Cleveland's Jim Bagby) and a remarkable performance of non-production by Brooklyn's Clarence Mitchell, who hit into the triple play and a double play in successive at-bats.

9. Game 2, 1916—For pitching fans, this one ranks with Larsen's perfect game. The Dodgers earned one run off Boston's Babe Ruth in the first; the Red Sox got it back off Brooklyn's Sherry Smith in the third. And that was all the scoring until the 14th, when Boston scratched a run to beat Smith as Ruth started a streak of 29 consecutive scoreless World Series innings.

10. Game 4, 1941—With two out, the Dodgers leading, 4-3, the bases empty and the count full on Tommy Henrich, pitcher Hugh Casey's curve/spitter eluded both Henrich, who swung and missed for strike three, and catcher Mickey Owen, who lunged and missed, allowing Henrich to reach first. The Yankees followed

with a four-run rally that was the turning point of the Series.

SOURCE: *Baseball Magazine*

Dick Enberg's 5 Most Memorable Games

Dick Enberg's assignments as an NBC sportscaster have ranged from Rose Bowl and Super Bowl to NCAA basketball, tennis at Wimbledon and, of course, big league baseball. Before becoming a full-time announcer, he was an associate professor and assistant baseball coach at California State-Northridge.

1. Nolan Ryan's no-hitter for the Angels against the Tigers on July 15, 1973. "Ryan had 18 strikeouts. I've never seen a human throw so hard. It was an absolutely awesome performance."
2. Rick Monday's ninth-inning homer against Montreal that won the 1981 pennant for the Dodgers. "It was Monday on Monday."
3. The explosive pre-game ceremonies (Angels vs. Yankees) that commemorated the 200th year of the U.S. Army at Shea Stadium in 1975. "The U.S. honor guard gave a 21-gun salute that literally blew down and set fire to the outfield fence."
4. The day in 1963 when Cal State-Northridge beat the USC freshmen, 7-6. "As frosh coach of a small school you rarely ever beat Rod Dedeaux' teams on any level."
5. Bobby Thomson's home run for the Giants that cost the Dodgers the pennant in 1951. "I wasn't there but I have used the film clip and Russ Hodges' famous call—'the Giants win the pennant, the Giants win the pennant, the Giants win the pennant . . .'—so many times on 'Sports Challenge' that I feel like I was there."

Donald Honig's 10 Greatest Teams

Donald Honig's list, which is chronological and not in order of preference, is from his book, *Baseball's 10 Greatest Teams,* published by Macmillan in 1982. Among other

UPI

Bobby Thomson, left; Jim Hearn, center, and Sal Maglie celebrate Thomson's pennant-winning homer against the Dodgers in 1951.

books, he wrote *Baseball When the Grass Was Real* and is the author of 11 novels.

1. The 1906 Chicago Cubs, who won 116 games (still a record) and featured the legendary Tinker to Evers to Chance.
2. The 1911 Philadelphia Athletics, with Connie Mack's $100,000 infield.
3. *The 1927 New York Yankees, led by Babe Ruth and Lou Gehrig.
4. The 1929-31 Philadelphia Athletics, featuring Lefty Grove and Jimmie Foxx.
5. The 1936 New York Yankees, with Lou Gehrig and a rookie named Joe DiMaggio.
6. The 1942 St. Louis Cardinals, with Enos Slaughter and a rookie named Stan Musial.
7. The 1953 Brooklyn Dodgers, with five .300 hitters.
8. The 1961 New York Yankees with Mickey Mantle and Roger Maris.
9. The 1969 Baltimore Orioles.
10. The 1976 Cincinnati Reds, "The Big Red Machine."

*The greatest team of all, according to author Honig.

Ray Robinson's 12 Greatest Stentors* of All Time

Loud mouths, or as they used to call them, bench jockeys.

Ray Robinson is editor of *Seventeen* magazine and a baseball typewriter jockey over the years who asks the question, "Whatever happened to that noble breed, the baseball bench jockey—those barbers, ribbers, baiters, needlers and joshers—who used to assail the enemy with thousands of uncomplimentary comments? Well, the strident hooligans of yesteryear seem to have turned into bevested businessmen-players of today. Pure and simple, they ain't what they used to be. If bench jockeying is, for the most part, extinct, then one of the fine arts, like illuminating manuscripts, has headed for the drain."

No. 1: Billy Martin needs no introduction.

Sports Photo Source

1. Billy Martin—Natch! The former fresh kid himself. One of the damnedest riders of them all. When he first came to the big leagues, they rode him unmercifully; he hasn't stopped giving it back.

2. Earl Weaver—A throwback to the past, a non-stop talker and walker, the premier umpire-baiter whose mouth has apparently helped him compile an enormous winning record as manager of the Baltimore Orioles.

3. Bill Rigney—Known as The Cricket, a talker-thinker who tried to emulate his predecessor as New York Giant manager, Lippy Leo Durocher.

4. Kurt Bevacqua (who?)—An infielder for San Diego and Pittsburgh who hasn't stopped talking yet after seven years or so of .210 hitting and no home runs.

5. Leo Durocher—Who else? He came out of the pool halls of West Springfield, Mass., to deliver some of the most stirring orations in the game's history. He dressed as loud as he talked. Once called the immortal Ty Cobb an "over-aged bum." To his face, yet.

6. Eddie Stanky—A Durocher disciple. He had all the intangibles, as Durocher said, including a gusty throat.

7. Jimmy Dykes—One of Connie Mack's favorites, never reluctant to pass up an opportunity to needle. Thrived on the Cleveland "Crybaby" rebellion of 1940.

8. Frankie Frisch—The hoarse old ringmaster of the St. Louis Gashouse Gang and a lover, surprisingly, of classical music and flowers.

9. Lefty Gomez—A Yankee pitcher with great humor and a wonderful winning percentage; a master of the baseball bon mot.

10. Whitey Ford—Another great Yankee southpaw, also with a penchant for delivering the needle with a pronounced New York accent.

11. John McGraw—The sawed-off bully boy who would hire private eyes in order to learn about the personal vexations of enemy pitchers. During the game, his players would then dwell lovingly on these afflictions.

12. Dizzy Dean—Pitched and punned his way to notoriety, a veritable squad of jockeys all by himself.

Robinson adds: "For the most part, racial and religious jockeying has ceased. So, some things do get better with time."

VI

The Toughest and the Worst

Eric Compton's 8 Rookies of the Year Who Succumbed to the Sophomore Jinx

Just being named the best rookie in baseball doesn't mean continued success in the big leagues. Who remembers Carl Morton? And what is Butch Metzger doing these days? Here are eight former Rookie-of-the-Year winners who had miserable seasons their second time around, as described by Eric Compton, a sportswriter on the New York *Daily News*.

1. Joe Charboneau, Cleveland Indians—In 1980, Charboneau tore up the American League, batting, .289 with 23 homers and 87 RBI. He spent most of the following season in the minor leagues, appearing in only 48 games with the Indians, batting .210 with four homers and 18 RBI.
2. Rick Sutcliffe, Los Angles Dodgers—Sutcliffe broke in with a bang, winning 17 and losing 10 with a 3.46 ERA for the Dodgers in 1979. But the sophomore jinx struck hard and he slumped to 3-9, 5.56 in 1980. He

has since been traded to the Indians, where he and Charboneau undoubtedly have swapped stories about what might have been.

3. Walt Dropo, Boston Red Sox—Enjoying one of the best rookie seasons in history, Dropo belted 34 homers and knocked in 144 runs while batting .322 for the 1950 Red Sox. It was a different story in 1951, however, as he fell off to 11 homers, 57 RBI and a .239 average.

4. Don Schwall, Boston Red Sox—Toast of the town to just another pitcher. Schwall won 14 of 21 decisions and had a 3.22 ERA in 1961 and even had three strong innings in the All-Star Game. The next year he slumped to 9-15 with a 4.95 ERA.

5. Harry Byrd, Philadelphia A's—Byrd soared in 1952, fell to earth in 1953. He won 15 games (while losing 15) for the A's his rookie season. In 1953, he was 11-20 with a 5.51 ERA. He never recaptured that Rookie-of-the-Year form.

6. Stan Bahnsen, New York Yankees—A flame thrower, Bahnsen was counted on to lead the Yankees back to glory in the late 1960s. He showed promise, going 17-12 with a 2.06 ERA in 1968. It was downhill after that, starting the slide with a 9-16 record and a 3.83 in his sophomore year.

7. Roy Sievers, St. Louis Browns—The American League's first Rookie of the Year in 1949, and he deserved it: 16 homers, 91 RBI, a .306 average. The sophomore jinx knocked him down to 10 homers, 57 RBI and .238 the next season.

8. Albie Pearson, Washington Senators—His jinx was so bad, he was traded early in his second season. In 1958, he batted .275 with three home runs and 33 RBI for the Senators. He was going so badly in 1959 that he was shipped to Baltimore, where he finished with no homers, only eight RBI and an anemic .216 average.

Note: Carl Morton, who was the 1970 NL winner with 18 triumphs for the hapless Montreal Expos, fell to 10-18 with a 4.79 ERA the following season. He never recovered his 1970 form. Butch Metzger, who shared the 1976 NL award with Pat Zachry of the Reds, shares another oddity with Zachry: they were both traded the year after winning the award.

It was a happy time in 1979 when Rick Sutcliffe was named Rookie of the Year, but it wasn't the same the following year.

UPI

Bobby Grich's 7 "Toughest Players I've Faced Sliding into Second to Break Up the Double Play"

1. Carlos May—"Strong and stocky, he slid in so high there was no way to jump out of his path."
2. Johnny Ellis—"Notorious for coming in hard."
3. Willie Wilson—"Perhaps the most feared. He's got good size, but more than that he's so fast that he's on you before you know it."
4. Reggie Jackson—"Again, size and speed."
5. and 6. George Brett and Hal McRae—"They're so competitive, in the late innings they become kamikaze-like in their efforts to wreck double plays."
7. Buddy Bell—"Big, and what a cross-body blocker."

SOURCE: *Inside Sports*

Al Clark's 5 Toughest Calls for an Umpire

Al Clark has been an American League umpire since 1976.

1. Batted ball curving around either left or right field foul pole for home run, or foul ball.
2. Half-swings at home plate.
3. Sliding tag plays at second base.
4. Calling balls and strikes on knuckleballs.
5. Traveling from one city to another in the morning and working that night.

Maury Wills' 3 Toughest Pitchers To Steal Against

1. Larry Jackson—"He had a natural balk move to first."
2. Warren Spahn
3. Juan Marichal

Note: Try as he might, Wills could only come up with three names when asked to name the toughest pitchers to steal against. "All the rest were easy," he said.

6 Least Desirable Cities for Major Leaguers

Since the advent of the Players Association, and later with free agency, players have greater control over where they will and will not play—no-trade clauses, veto on trades, right of refusal, etc. Players tend to gravitate toward major markets (New York, L.A.), winning teams (Yankees, Dodgers, Brewers, Phillies) and warmer climates (California, Texas). They also have generally refused to play in some cities.

1. Minneapolis—No one wants to play for Calvin Griffith, who maintains the lowest payroll in the game.
2. Toronto—Canadian tax laws are prohibitive.
3. Montreal—Ditto.
4. Cleveland—Because it's Cleveland.
5. Seattle—Small, indoor ballpark, plus non-contender and too close to Mt. St. Helen's.
6. San Francisco—Great city by the bay, but those winds at Candlestick make it undesirable.

Red Foley's 10 Baseball Records That Will Never Be Broken

A genuine historian on the grand, old game, Red Foley regularly writes a column, "Ask Red," for the New York *Daily News,* in which he answers baseball questions from fans.

1. Lou Gehrig's 2,130 consecutive-game streak.
2. Johnny Vander Meer's two consecutive no-hit games.
3. Cy Young's 511 career major league victories.
4. Connie Mack's 50 years managing the same club.
5. Rogers Hornsby's composite five-year batting average of .402 (1921-25).

UPI

Babe Ruth was on the scene at Ebbets Field on the night in 1938 when Cincinnati's Johnny Vander Meer pitched his second consecutive no-hitter.

6. Consecutive .400 seasons, Ty Cobb (1911-12) and Rogers Hornsby (1924-25).
7. Joe DiMaggio's 56-game hitting streak.
8. Jack Chesbro's 41 pitching victories in 1904.
9. Most consecutive innings pitched without relief: John W. Taylor, Chicago Cubs and St. Louis Cardinals, 203, June 20, 1901 through August 9, 1906.
10. Bill Dahlen's career record of 972 errors at shortstop over 20 years, covering 2,139 games.

Foley adds: "Two consecutive no-hitters, not an impossibility, would only equal Vander Meer's record. To break his record, a pitcher must pitch three consecutive no-hitters; Dahlen averaged 48.6 errors a season but because of better equipment (gloves), fielders don't miss as many balls, and these days a player would be replaced if he even got close to Dahlen's record."

The 10 Worst Teams in Baseball History

1. Philadelphia A's, 1916—The 1916 season was unique in American League history. Six clubs finished at .500 and above, and the seventh-place Washington Senators came home with a respectable .497 percentage. Front-running Boston and the six other successful clubs were able to manage such evenly balanced records because of the performance of Connie Mack's atrocious A's, 36-117, 40 games out of first place. A year earlier, Mack had dismantled a championship team, although he retained pitcher Bullet Joe Bush, who won 15 of his team's 36 games, eight by shutout. Elmer Myles won 13. Johnny Nabors started the season with a victory, then dropped 19 in a row. Tom Sheehan was 1-16, Jing Johnson 2-10. Shortstop Whitey Witt made 78 errors; third baseman Charlie Peck kicked in with 42 more.
2. Boston Beaneaters, 1906—This team had four 20-game losers: Irv Young, Gus Dorner, Vive Lindaman and Jeff Pfeffer. A 19-game losing streak "helped" the Beanies finish 66½ games behind the pennant-winning Cubs, the largest margin in baseball history.

3. Boston Braves, 1935—Wally Berger led the National League with 34 homers and 130 RBI, and a teammate was Babe Ruth (age 40 and winding down his career), but the Braves still finished with a record of 38-115, 61½ games out of first place.

4. New York Mets, 1962—The Amazin' Mets of Casey Stengel were easily the most laughable, most scoffed-at team in baseball history, winning 40 games and losing 120 in the first year of their existence. They had losing streaks of 13 and 17 games, and once scored 18 runs in a game, prompting one beleaguered Met fan to inquire: "Did they win?"

5. Pittsburgh Pirates, 1952—Catcher Joe Garagiola described this as "the ninth year of (GM) Branch Rickey's five-year plan." The Pirates finished 42-112, 54½ games out of first, despite the presence of Hall of Famer Ralph Kiner, who belted 37 homers. The Bucs used 16 men in their starting rotation, and the staff walked 615 batters and struck out only 564.

6. St. Louis Browns, 1939—Jack Kramer and Vern Kennedy led the staff with nine victories each for a team that finished 43-111, a record 64½ games behind the leader.

7. Philadelphia's A's, 1919—With a pitching staff that had a combined ERA of 4.26 and posted just one shutout, the A's had a 36-104 record, 52 games out of first.

8. Philadelphia Phillies, 1942—The best hitter for this team of castoffs, has-beens and never-weres was Danny Litwhiler, who posted mediocre stats of .271, nine homers, and 56 RBI in "leading" the Phillies to a 42-109 finish, 62½ games behind the pace-setting Cardinals.

9. Philadelphia Phillies, 1961—Hall of Famer Robin Roberts entered the 1961 season with 233 career victories and finished the season with 234. This was the nucleus of a potential National League power, but it suffered from growing pains, including a record 23-game losing streak under rookie manager Gene Mauch. The Phillies finished with a record of 47-107, 46 games off the lead.

10. St. Louis Cardinals, 1908—Pitching, they say, is 75 percent of baseball. Not in the case of this team,

which had a staff ERA of 2.64. Still, the Cards ended with a record of 49-105, 50 games out of first, because they could not hit. Three regulars batted under .200, and the Cards were shut out 33 times during the regular season, or once in every five games.

SOURCE: *Baseball Magazine*

The Yankees' Rich Gossage is a toughie for Rod Carew.

Mitchell B. Reibel

VII

On the Mound

Rod Carew's 10 Toughest Pitchers To Hit

1. Nolan Ryan
2. Rudy May
3. Ron Guidry
4. Mickey Lolich
5. Dave McNally
6. Rich Gossage
7. Sam McDowell
8. Sparky Lyle
9. Steve Hargan
10. Mel Stottlemyre

SOURCE: Dick Miller, formerly of the Los Angeles *Herald-Examiner,* who says: ''Rod got through the first five pretty easily, then had trouble coming up with the rest, saying, 'I can't think of too many other guys.' You'll note after Nolan Ryan, the next four and six of seven are lefthanders. At one time, when I did a column on him, I checked and Carew was batting .303 against Ryan, which indicates how good a hitter he is. Rodney says he rates Ryan No. 1 on the basis of stuff and still maintains he never has felt fear batting against anyone, including Ryan.''

As an Angel, Nolan Ryan is en route to his fourth no-hitter, against the
Orioles, in 1975.

UPI

Note: Entering the 1983 season, Carew's lifetime batting
average was .331, by far the highest among active players
and 23rd on the all-time list despite the fact that batting
averages have decreased dramatically in the last four decades.

9 Rookie Pitchers Who Won Strikeout Crowns

1. Dazzy Vance, Brooklyn, 1922
2. Lefty Grove, Philadelphia, AL, 1925
3. Dizzy Dean, St. Louis, NL, 1932
4. Allie Reynolds, Cleveland, 1943
5. Bill Voiselle, New York, NL, 1944
6. Herb Score, Cleveland, 1955
7. Sam Jones, Chicago, NL, 1955
8. Jack Sanford, San Francisco, 1957
9. Fernando Valenzuela, Los Angeles, 1981

10 Rookie Pitchers Who Struck Out 200 Batters

1. Tom Hughes, Chicago, NL, 1901
2. Christy Mathewson, New York, NL, 1901
3. Russ Ford, New York, AL, 1910
4. Grover Cleveland Alexander, Philadelphia, NL, 1911
5. Herb Score, Cleveland, 1955
6. Don Sutton, Los Angeles, NL, 1966
7. Gary Nolan, Cincinnati, 1967
8. Tom Griffin, Houston, 1969
9. Bob Johnson, Kansas City, 1970
10. John Montefusco, San Francisco, 1975

5 Pitchers Rescued by Famous World Series Catches

1. Joe Hatten—Dodger Al Gionfriddo's catch of Joe Di-Maggio's drive to the Yankee Stadium bullpen in 1947.
2. Bob Kuzava—Yankee Billy Martin's fingertip grab of Dodger Jackie Robinson's bases-loaded, two-out popup after a long run in 1952.
3. Don Liddle—New York Giant Willie Mays' back-to-the-plate catch of Indian Vic Wertz' 440-foot drive with two on and the score tied in Game 1 in 1954.
4. Tom Seaver—Met Ron Swoboda's diving grab of Oriole Brooks Robinson's ninth-inning bid for a triple in 1969.
5. Tug McGraw—Phillie Pete Rose's lunging snare of Royal Frank White's popup, which had glanced off the glove of catcher Bob Boone with bases loaded and one out in the ninth inning of the sixth and final game in 1980.

SOURCE: Frank Kelly of the New York *Daily News*

10 Pitchers Whose No-Hit Games Are Rarely Talked About

One of the rarest of baseball feats is the no-hit game. It has been computed that odds against a pitcher pitching a no-hitter are 1,300-to-1. According to Jack Little, a member of the Society for American Baseball Research, "You would think that someone who performed such a feat would be a star; at least well remembered. When most people think of no-hit pitchers, they think of people like Sandy Koufax, Bob Feller or Nolan Ryan. But that's not always the case and I hereby present 10 pitchers of no-hit games who aren't household names."

1. Charles (Bumpus) Jones—Had a lifetime record of 2-4 and the no-hitter represented half his major league victory total. Pitching for Cincinnati, Jones held Pittsburgh hitless for a 7-1 victory in his first major league game on October 15, 1892. The following season, he was 1-3 with Cincinnati, then was traded to New York. By 1894, he was out of the major leagues.

2. August Weyhing—His lifetime record was 264-234 pitching for 10 teams in four leagues over a 14-year career that ended in 1901. He was very much in demand in the 1880s and 1890s. Pitched his no-hitter for Philadelphia of the American Association on July 31, 1888, beating Kansas City, 4-0.

3. George Washington (Grin) Bradley—He pitched the first National League no-hitter for St. Louis against Hartford on July 15, 1876, the NL's inaugural season. You rarely hear it mentioned that he was the first. However, one year earlier, Joseph Borden, also known as Joseph Emley Josephs, pitched the first recorded no-hitter on July 28, 1875, when he defeated Chicago for Philadelphia, 4-0. But that was in the old National Association, in the Dark Ages of the sport.

4. Frank Smith—Pitched two no-hitters, beating Detroit, 15-0, for Chicago on September 6, 1905, and topping Philadelphia, 1-0, also for Chicago on September 20, 1908.

5. Samuel Kimber—Pitched 10 perfect innings for Brooklyn against Toledo on October 4, 1884, but didn't even have a victory to show for his efforts. The game was called because of darkness after 10 innings with the score 0-0.

6. Paul Dean—His better known brother, Dizzy, pitched a two-hitter in the first game of a doubleheader against Brooklyn on September 21, 1934. Paul pitched the

second game and completed a sweep of the double-header for the St. Louis Cardinals with his 3-0 no-hitter. After the second game, Dizzy greeted his kid brother. ''Now that's real Dean pitchin','' chirped Dizzy. ''But why didn't you tell me you wuz gonna pitch a no-hitter, Paul, cause I'da pitched one, too.'' Dizzy won 150 games in the major leagues but never pitched a no-hitter. His brother Paul, who won 50 games, did.

7. Jim Wilson—Fractured his skull in 1945. Nine years later, on June 12, 1954, he no-hit the Phillies, 2-0, for the Milwaukee Braves.

8. George Davis—His no-hitter came on September 9, 1914, a 7-0 victory for Boston over Philadelphia. But that was the year of the ''Miracle Braves,'' who went from last place on July 4 to win the pennant and the team's performance overshadowed all individual achievements.

9. Albert Atkisson—Pitched no-hitters in both the American Association (for Philadelphia vs. Pittsburgh on May 24, 1884) and the National League (for Philadelphia vs. New York on May 1, 1886).

10. Dick Fowler—Returned from the Armed Forces late in the 1945 season to win one game and lose two for the Philadelphia Athletics. That one victory was his gem, a 1-0 no-hitter on September 9 against the St. Louis Browns.

11 Great Pickoff Pitchers, or Pitchers Who Dissuaded Runners from Stealing Bases because of Motions That Kept Them Close

1. Bill Wight
2. Hughie McQuillen
3. Whitey Ford
4. Warren Spahn
5. Larry Jackson
6. Frank Lary
7. Don Drysdale
8. Clyde King
9. Art Mahaffey

10. Sherry Smith
11. Roger Craig

SOURCE: Red Foley

7 Pitchers Who Never Got Anybody Out in Their Major League Careers

1. Joe Brown, Chicago (AL), 1927
2. Fred Bruckbauer, Minnesota, 1961
3. Doc Hermann, Cleveland, 1922
4. Willis Koenigmark, St. Louis (NL), 1919
5. Bill Moore, Detroit, 1925
6. Mike Palagyi, Washington, 1939
7. Jim Schelle, Philadelphia (AL), 1939

5 Pitchers Who Won 20 Games or More at Age 40

	Year	W-L
1. Cy Young, Boston, (AL), 1907		22-15
2. Grover Cleveland Alexander, St. Louis (NL), 1927		21-10
3. Gaylord Perry, San Diego, 1978		21-6
4. Warren Spahn, Milwaukee, (NL), 1961		21-15
5. Phil Niekro, Atlanta, 1979		21-20

9 Pitchers Who Pitched Only One-Third of an Inning in the Major Leagues

1. Eddie Ainsmith, Washington, 1913
2. Ted Cather, St. Louis (NL), 1913
3. Joe Cleary, Washington, 1945
4. Marc Filley, Washington, 1934
5. Fritz Fisher, Detroit, 1964
6. Art Goodwin, New York (AL), 1905
7. Harley Grossman, Washington, 1952
8. Jim Mosolf, Pittsburgh, 1930
9. Fran Wurm, Brooklyn, 1944

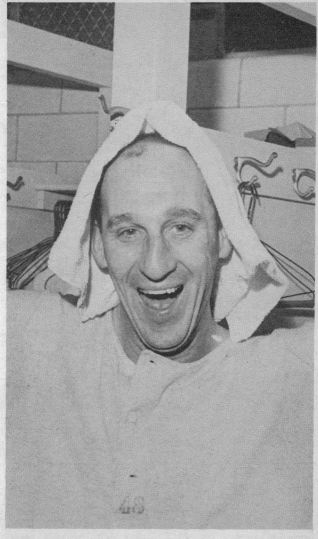

Warren Spahn, at age 40, celebrates his second no-hitter, against San Francisco, in 1961.

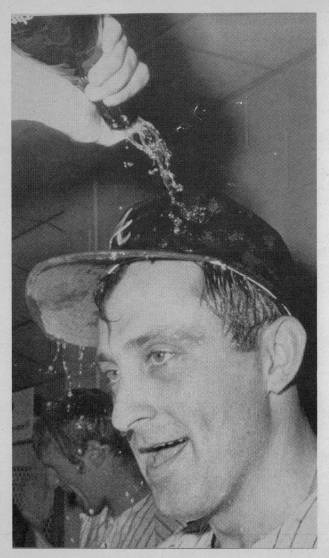

As a 40-year-old, Phil Niekro won 21 games.

UPI

All-Time Listing of the Winningest Pitchers Whose Names Begin with Each Letter of the Alphabet, 1900-1982

A—Grover Cleveland Alexander, 373
B—Mordecai "Three Finger" Brown, 239
C—Steve Carlton, 262
D—Paul Derringer, 223
E—Howard Ehmke, 167
F—Bob Feller, 266
G—Lefty Grove, 300
H—Carl Hubbell, 253
I—Ham Iburg, 11
J—Walter Johnson, 416
K—Jim Kaat, 283
L—Ted Lyons, 260
M—Christy Mathewson, 373
N—Phil Niekro, 257
O—Claude Osteen, 196
P—Ed Plank, 325
Q—Jack Quinn, 241
R—Robin Roberts, 286
S—Warren Spahn, 363
T—Luis Tiant, 229
U—George Uhle, 200
V—Dazzy Vance, 197
W—Early Wynn, 300
X—
Y—Cy Young, 511
Z—Tom Zachary, 185

Most Lifetime Relief Appearances without Ever Starting a Game (Through 1982)

1. Sparky Lyle 854
2. Bob Locker 576
3. Kent Tekulve ...571
4. Jack Aker 495
5. Joe Hoerner 493
6. Jack Baldschun .457

7. Wayne Granger .451
8. Dick Radatz 381
T9. Bruce Sutter 348
T9. Cecil Upshaw ... 348

Keith Olbermann's 10 Top World Series Pitching Performances

1. Christy Mathewson, 1905—The Giants' ace set an unbeatable record, shutting out the A's three times in five days. Mathewson pitched two four-hitters and a six-hitter, struck out 18 and walked one.
2. Don Larsen, 1956—What Mathewson was to one Series, Larsen was to one game—his unblemished effort against the Dodgers standing a quarter of a century later as the only World Series perfect game or no-hitter.
3. Babe Ruth, 1916—Ruth's 14-inning, 2-1 duel with

His teammates congratulate Bob Gibson after his 17-strikeout performance in the 1968 World Series.

Malcolm Emmons

Babe Ruth set a World Series pitching mark with the Red Sox.

UPI

Sherry Smith was the start of a streak of 29 consecutive scoreless innings in World Series pitching for the game's most celebrated home run hitter.

4. Moe Drabowsky, 1966—Relieving Dave McNally in the third inning of the opener of the Orioles-Dodgers series, this journeyman pitcher struck out 11 in six and two-thirds innings, six consecutively to tie the Series mark.

5. Bob Gibson, 1964-67-68—Gibson won twice for the

Cardinals in 1964; won three times, one by shutout, in 1967 and won two more in 1968, setting the record of 17 strikeouts against Detroit in Game 1 in 1968. Twice he won the seventh game for his team.

6. Whitey Ford, 1960-61—The Yankee lefthander pitched three straight Series shutouts, beating the Pirates twice in 1960 and blanking the Reds in the opener of the 1961 series, later setting the World Series record of 32 consecutive scoreless innings.

7. Lew Burdette, 1957—Gaining revenge on the club that traded him away, Burdette pitched three complete game victories and two shutouts as the Braves defeated the Yankees.

8. Babe Adams, 1909—This unheralded rookie won three times as the Pirates beat the Tigers.

9. Larry Sherry, 1959—Another rookie, he won two games in relief and saved two others for the Dodgers against the White Sox.

10. Mickey Lolich, 1968—The last pitcher to win three games in one Series, Lolich upstaged 31-game winner Denny McLain as Detroit beat St. Louis in 1968, topping Bob Gibson in the seventh game.

SOURCE: *Baseball Magazine*

VIII

Through the Ages

Dr. Creighton J. Hale's 9 Most Memorable Moments in Little League World Series

Dr. Creighton J. Hale is president of Little League Baseball.

1. First perfect game pitched by Angel Macias, Monterrey, Mexico, in 1957, following by 10 months the first major league World Series perfect game by Don Larsen. Macias beat LaMesa, California, 4-0.
2. Championship team from Monterrey, Mexico, hosted by three men who were, or were to become, presidents of the United States—President Dwight D. Eisenhower, Vice President Richard M. Nixon, Senate majority leader Lyndon B. Johnson. The meetings of the 1957 World Championship team from Mexico with Eisenhower, Nixon and Johnson took place in Washington, D.C. President Eisenhower received the team in the Oval Office of the White House and Vice President Nixon and Senate Majority Leader Johnson later hosted the team at a luncheon.
3. The largest player in Series history, Ted Campbell, a 6-1, 210-pound, 12-year-old pitcher from San Jose,

Ted Campbell, a 6-1, 210-pound, 12-year-old, towers over all at the Little League World Series in 1962.

Little League

California, pitched a no-hit, no-run game against Kankakee, IL, in 1962.
4. Arthur Deras of Hamtramck, MI., in two games gave up four hits, struck out 30 batters and pitched scoreless ball in 1959.
5. Championship game telecast to the Far East via Telstar in 1970.
6. Lloyd McClendon, in two games, batted five-for-five, all home runs, in 1971.
7. Yankee Clipper Joe DiMaggio was asked by a player prior to the championship game in 1976 to sign a baseball "Mr. Coffee."
8. Jay Herring of Little Rock, AK, competed in the 1979 Series 26 years after his father, James, played in the Series.

9. Red Barber and Mel Allen provided the play-by-play of the championship game on ABC's Wide World of Sports in 1979.

Steve Kenner's 8 Unusual Little League Graduates

Steve Keener is Little League Baseball's assistant director of public relations.

1. Mike Schmidt—Played in the North Riverdale Little League, Dayton, Ohio. He has developed from Little Leaguer to the best all-around player in the game today.
2. Steve Garvey—Played in the Drew Park Little League, Tampa, Fla. Steve exemplifies most how a wholesome activity such as Little League can develop outstanding character and be a road to greatness.
3. George Foster—Played in the Tri-Park Little League, Lawndale, Cal. George is a favorite and not so much for the home runs he hits, but rather for his dedication to the "Building Bridges" program to help troubled youngsters.
4. Mike Eruzione—Played in the Winthrop Little League, Winthrop, Mass. Mike captained the United States hockey team that beat the Russians and Finns to win the 1980 Olympic gold medal, sending a wave of new-found patriotism across the country.
5. Gary Carter—Played in the West Fullerton Little League, Fullerton, Cal. Gary ranks high on my list for passing up a television interview prior to a 1981 game to give a few minutes to Little League.
6. Ken Landreaux—Played in the Compton American Little League, Compton, Cal. Ken was the 1980 recipient of the Aqua Velva consecutive-game hitting-streak award, having hit safely in 31 straight games. He donated half of his $31,000 prize to his former Little League.
7. Kareem Abdul-Jabbar—Played in the Inwood Little League, New York City. Kareem is a sentimental favorite because of his 6-2, 12-year-old frame which would not permit one piece of his uniform to fit properly, but mostly because he is considered by many to be the greatest player in the history of basketball.
8. Jimmy Lopez—Played in the Globe Little League, Globe,

Ariz. Jimmy was held hostage in Iran for 444 days and was directly responsible for getting five Americans to safety in the Canadian Embassy before being captured.

Satchel Paige's 6 Steps to Eternal Youth

1. Avoid fried meats, which angry up the blood.
2. If your stomach disputes you, lie down and pacify it with cool thoughts.
3. Keep the juices flowing by jangling around gently as you move.
4. Go very light on the vices, such as carrying on in society. The social rumble ain't restful.
5. Avoid running at all times.
6. Don't look back. Something might be gaining on you.

Note: Satchel Paige, called "the greatest pitcher who ever lived" by Dizzy Dean, was the legendary star of baseball's Negro Leagues. He made the major leagues with the Cleveland Indians in 1949, when he was said to be 42 years old, at least. He pitched three innings for the Kansas City A's in 1965, making him, presumably at age 59, the oldest man to pitch in the major leagues. Of his six rules, Paige calls No. 6 "My real rule. When you look back, you know how long you've been going and that just might stop you from going any farther. And with me, there was an awful lot to look back on. So I didn't." Paige was elected to the Baseball Hall of Fame in 1971.

Herman L. Masin's All-Time New York City High School Baseball Team, Featuring 6—Count 'Em—Hall of Famers, Which Must Be a Record for One City

As editor of *Scholastic Coach*, Herman Masin has been keeping tabs on the nation's outstanding high school sports stars for more than four decades.

1b—Lou Gehrig, Commerce H.S.
2b—Frank Frisch, Fordham Prep
3b—Frank Malzone, Samuel Gompers H.S.
 ss—Phil Rizzuto, Richmond Hill H.S.
 of—Hank Greenberg, James Monroe H.S.
 of—Rocky Colavito, Roosevelt H.S.
 of—Tommy Davis, Boys H.S.
dh—Rod Carew, George Washington H.S.
dh—Frank McCormick, St. Monica's
 c—Joe Torre, St. Francis Prep
 p—Sandy Koufax, Lafayette H.S.
 p—Whitey Ford, Manhattan Aviation
 p—Waite Hoyt, Erasmus Hall H.S.
official clown—Al Schacht, Commerce H.S.

Herman L. Masin's All-Time Italian Stallion New York City High School Baseball Team . . . and May Phil Rizzuto Forever Hold His Peace

1b—Joe Pepitone, Manual Training H.S.
2b—Ken Aspromonte, Lafayette H.S.
3b—Frank Malzone, Samuel Gompers H.S.
 ss—Phil Rizzuto, Richmond Hill H.S.
 of—Rocky Colavito, Roosevelt H.S.
 of—Lee Mazzilli, Lincoln H.S.
 of—Sam Mele, Bryant H.S.
 c—Joe Torre, St. Francis Prep
 p—Marius Russo, Richmond Hill H.S.
official biographer—Phil Pepe, Lafayette H.S.

Houston Colts' All-Kiddie Lineup

1b—Rusty Staub, 19
2b—Joe Morgan, 20
3b—Glenn Vaughn, 19
 ss—Sonny Jackson, 19
 lf—Brock Davis, 19
cf—Jimmy Wynn, 21
rf—Aaron Pointer, 21
 c—Jerry Grote, 20
 p—Jay Dahl, 17

Note: This lineup took the field on September 27, 1963.

Submitted by L. Robert Davids, SABR

11 Oldest Players to Appear in a Minor League Game

Player and Pos.	Team	League	Year	Age
1. Hub Kittle, p	Springfield	Amer. Assn.	1980	63
2. Satchel Paige, p	Peninsula	Carolina	1966	60
3. Lefty O'Doul, ph	Vancouver	PCL	1956	59
4. Lefty George, p	York	NY-Penn	1944	57
5. Jim O'Rourke, 1b	Bridgeport	Conn.	1907	55
6. Bill McCorry, p	Ogden	Pioneer	1942	55
7. Joe McGinnity, p	Dubuque	Miss. Valley	1925	54
8. Herb Brett, p	Winston-Salem	Carolina	1954	54
9. Pepper Martin, pr	Tulsa	Texas	1958	54
10. John McCloskey, ph	El Paso	Rio Grande Valley	1915	53
11. Charles Shaney, p	Asheville	Carolina	1954	53

Doug Huff's 8 Major Leaguers with Outstanding High School Feats

Doug Huff, sports editor of the Wheeling (WV) *Intelligencer,* is one of the nation's foremost authorities on high school sports.

1. J. R. Richard ended the 1969 season at Lincoln High of Ruston, La., with a spotless 0.00 earned-run average and also had a four-home run, 10-RBI game.
2. Hall of Famer Walter Johnson struck out 27 batters in a 1905 game for Fullerton (Cal.) High.
3. Sixty-two years after Johnson, Vida Blue got all 21 outs on strikeouts in a seven-inning game for DeSoto High of Mansfield, La.
4. Paul Richards, a major league catcher and manager, pitched his Waxahachie, Tex., team to victory in both ends of a doubleheader in 1927—one righthanded, the other lefthanded. From 1925-27, Waxahachie won 65 consecutive games with six players on the roster who

later played in the major leagues—Richards, Art Shires, Gene Moore, Jimmy Adair, Archie Wise and Belve Bean.

5. Scott McGregor was the stopper for El Segundo, Cal., High with a career record of 51-6 from 1970 through 1972.

6. Floyd Bannister duplicated J. R. Richard's unblemished ERA season for Kennedy High of Seattle, Wash., in 1973 and ended his career with an 0.56 ERA.

7. Terry Francona, son of ex-major leaguer Tito Francona, batted .769 for New Brighton, Pa., in 1976.

8. Andy Kosco wasn't far behind Francona with a .700 season average for Struthers, Colo., in 1959.

Doug Huff's 9 Remarkable High School Performances

1. Two Oklahoma pitchers combined for 72 strikeouts in a 17-inning game in 1971. Billy Brimm of Asher whiffed 37 in the 10-4 victory, while Joey Edelton of Gracemont struck out 35 in defeat.

2. Joey Porter of Adams High in South Natchez, Miss., didn't need many runs to win games in 1973. He hurled 11 consecutive shutouts and had a string of 80 consecutive scoreless innings.

3. Gary Rowe and Tom Murray went one step farther than Porter. Each hurled five consecutive no-hitters. Rowe did it for Wagoner, Okla., in 1977. Murray spread his over two seasons, 1968 and 1969, for St. Bernard High of Uncasville, Conn.

4. Opposing teams found the pitching star of Edgewood High in West Covina, Cal., a bitter pill to swallow from 1975 through 1977. Mike Pill was unbeaten in 33 consecutive decisions.

5. Another California schoolboy, Shane Mack of Gehr High, opened some eyes in 1981 when he belted out 16 consecutive hits over a five-game tear.

6. David Clyde was drafted by the Texas Rangers right out of Westchester High in Houston, Tex., where he hurled 115 consecutive scoreless innings in 1972 and 95 consecutive scoreless innings in 1973. Clyde also struck out 327 batters in one season and 842 in his high

school career, during which he won 53 games, pitched 29 shutouts (13 in one season) and 10 no-hitters.

7. Melvin Begley of Boise City, Okla., was a batting terror in 1953-54 with a career batting average of .727 and a single-season average of .806 in his senior year.

8. Vince Meyer has coached St. John High of Bancroft, Iowa, to 1,200 victories, 32 state playoffs and six Iowa 1-A championships in a 45-year career.

9. Ken Beardslee of Vermontville, Mich., averaged 19 strikeouts a game (209 in 11 games) in 1949, and his career average was 18.1 per start from 1947-49 (452 strikeouts in 25 games).

19 Players Who Hit 40 Home Runs in One Season at Age 25 or Younger

Player	Age	Year	Homers
1. Mel Ott	20	1929	42
2. Eddie Mathews	21	1953	47
3. Joe DiMaggio	22	1937	46
4. Hank Aaron	23	1957	44
5. Willie Mays	23	1954	41
6. Hal Trosky	23	1936	42
7. Reggie Jackson	23	1969	47
8. Harmon Killebrew	23	1959	42
9. Lou Gehrig	24	1927	47
10. Chuck Klein	24	1929	43
11. Ralph Kiner	24	1947	51
12. Ernie Banks	24	1955	44
13. Dick Allen	24	1966	40
14. Willie McCovey	25	1963	44
15. Rocky Colavito	25	1958	41
16. Jim Rice	25	1978	46
17. Mickey Mantle	25	1956	52
18. Babe Ruth	25	1920	54
19. Jimmie Foxx	25	1932	58

SOURCE: *Baseball Digest*

Mel Ott, who first reported to the Giants when he was 16 years old, belted 42 homers when he was 20.

UPI

Eddie Mathews was only 21, in his second season in the majors, when he clouted 47 homers for the Milwaukee Braves in 1953. That was the most homers he would hit in a single season over a prodigious 17-year career.

UPI

20 Graduates of Los Angeles' Fremont High Who Played in the Major Leagues

1. Bobby Doerr
2. Hal Spindel
3. Ed Stewart
4. Merrill Combs
5. George Metkovich
6. Gene Mauch
7. Clint Conatser
8. Nippy Jones
9. Dick Conger
10. Glenn Mickens
11. Al Grunwald
12. Willie Crawford
13. Bobby Tolan
14. Bob Watson
15. Brock Davis
16. George Hendrick

17. Leon McFadden
18. Alonzo Harris
19. Dan Ford
20. Chet Lemon

Submitted by Rick Obrand, SABR

Baseball's 5 Biggest Bonus Baby Flops

1. Billy Joe Davidson—The Cleveland Indians paid a reported $120,000 to sign Billy Joe after an outstanding high school career in which he averaged almost 19 strikeouts a game. Davidson never made it to the majors. The highest level of professional ball he reached was Cedar Rapids, a class B club, where his record was 1-5.
2. Bob Taylor—The Milwaukee Braves shelled out $100,000 for this promising young catcher who batted .218 in 394 major league games over 11 seasons.
3. Frank Baumann—The Boston Red Sox reportedly paid $125,000 for this hot prospect who won 45 games in 11 seasons. He did win ERA crown with White Sox in 1960.
4. Bobby Guindon—The Red Sox paid $125,000 for this budding star. Guindon appeared in five games in 1964. He went one-for-eight, a .125 average, and struck out four times.
5. Paul Pettit—In January 1950, the Pittsburgh Pirates paid $100,000 for this young pitcher. Pettit made brief appearances in 1951 and 1953. His career stats are 1-2, a 7.34 ERA, 21 walks, 14 strikeouts in 30⅔ innings.

Submitted by Jeff C. Young, Lebanon, Ind.

2 Players Who Played in Five Decades and 15 Players Who Played in Four Decades

Listed are the players' first and last clubs and the years their careers began and ended.

Ted Williams, a four-decade performer, gives tips to a rookie named Carl Yastrzemski in 1961.

UPI

Five Decades

1. Nick Altrock, Louisville, NL, 1898—Washington, AL, 1933*
2. Minnie Minoso, Cleveland, AL, 1949—Chicago, AL, 1980*

Four Decades

1. James O'Rourke, Boston, NL, 1876—New York, NL, 1904*
2. Dan Brouthers, Troy, NL, 1879—New York, NL, 1904*
3. Deacon McGuire, Toledo, AA, 1884—Detroit, AL, 1912*
4. Jack O'Connor, Cincinnati, AA, 1887—St. Louis, AL, 1910*
5. Kid Gleason, Philadelphia, NL, 1888—Chicago, AL, 1912*
6. John Ryan, Louisville, AA, 1889—Washington, AL, 1913*

7. Eddie Collins, Philadelphia, AL, 1906-Philadelphia, AL, 1930*

8. Jack Quinn, New York, AL, 1909—Cincinnati, NL, 1933

9. Bobo Newsom, Brooklyn, NL, 1929—Philadelphia, AL, 1953

10. Ted Williams, Boston, AL, 1939—Boston, AL, 1960

11. Mickey Vernon, Washington, AL, 1939—Pittsburgh, NL, 1960*

12. Early Wynn, Washington, AL, 1939—Cleveland, AL, 1963

13. Willie McCovey, San Francisco, NL, 1959—San Francisco, NL, 1980

14. Tim McCarver, St. Louis, NL, 1959—Philadelphia, NL, 1980*

15. Jim Kaat, Washington, AL, 1959—St. Louis, NL, 1982

*Denotes token appearance

Submitted by Ted DiTullio, SABR, who adds: "As can be seen from the above, most of the players made little more than token appearances in their final year. In fact, Minnie Minoso made a token appearance in 1976 to qualify as a four-decade player and again in 1980 to qualify as a five-decade player. Tim McCarver was only 38 when he qualified in September, 1980, as a four-decade player. Ted Williams probably made the biggest impression at both ends of the spectrum, being an all-star in 1939 and a near regular with 29 home runs in 1960.

Babe Ruth would have had a ball in the Boston Marathon.

UPI

IX

Playing Another Game

Ray Fitzgerald's Fantasy on How 8 Baseball Greats Would Run the Boston Marathon

1. Babe Ruth would have 26 hot dogs and 387 beers and finish up with a picnic lunch along the Charles.
2. Hank Aaron would go unnoticed for 21 miles and suddenly would appear three miles ahead of everyone else on the Newton Hills.
3. Ty Cobb would spike three judges, rip five kids off their bicycles and stuff a rubber hose down the throat of a spectator trying to give him Gatorade.
4. Reggie Jackson would drive a silver Phaeton to the Hopkinton starting line, demand uniform No. 1 and hold a press conference to discuss the psychological ramifications of the marathon as related to the cosmic whole.
5. Ted Williams would spit at the press bus.
6. Pete Rose would run the distance five times.
7. Shoeless Joe Jackson would appear from behind a tree in Brookline and a small kid would yell, "Say it ain't so, Joe."

8. Casey Stengel would get to the Happy Swallow bar in Framingham Centre and tell stories for the rest of the afternoon, and you could look it up.

Battling Billy Martin's 3 Favorite Fighters among Baseball Players

1. Gene Conley
2. Eddie Mathews
3. Willie Horton

Submitted by Dave Newhouse

Battling Billy Martin's 6 Favorite Boxers

1. Jack Dempsey
2. Joe Louis
3. Sugar Ray Robinson
4. Willie Pep
5. Rocky Marciano
6. Jack Johnson

Submitted by Dave Newhouse

Ted Williams' 2 Favorite Fishing Holes in the World

"The Splendid Splinter," Ted Williams, the last major league batter to hit .400 (.406 in 1941), is a renowned fisherman who owns more than 5,000 hooks and is on the Sears Advisory Board. Modest about his baseball career, he is justifiably proud of his record as a fisherman. When jazz saxophonist Flip Phillips was introduced to Williams, the latter was described as "the greatest hitter who ever lived."

"I don't know about that," Williams said, according to Phillips, "but I do know I'm the greatest fisherman who ever lived."

Famed heavyweight champ Jack Dempsey, left, No. 1 on Billy Martin's list, shares a reunion with his celebrated rival, Gene Tunney.

UPI

1. Miramichi River, Blackville, New Brunswick, Canada (Atlantic salmon).
2. Florida waters off Islamorada in the Florida Keys (bonefish).

Note: The above are listed because his home is Islamorada and he spends winters and most of his springs and falls there, then goes to Blackville in the summer.

Says Williams: "During the course of the year, I fish out of a dozen or more of some of the most fabulous fishing spots known to man. It is impossible to list them.

"I can truthfully say that my fishing jaunts have taken me to nearly all parts of the world. I've enjoyed days of fishing in Yucatan, Peru, British Columbia, most of the top places in North and South America. I've thoroughly covered the United States and found some of the best fishing in Wisconsin, and the Florida Keys, as well as Costa Rica, the West Indies, New Zealand, Australia, and others too numerous to mention.

"I enjoy fishing for sailfish, tarpon, trout, bass, and other species, but I have to say that standing in the waters of the Miramichi River, waist-high and in hip boots, waiting for the Atlantic salmon to bite or tug at my line, is my idea of enjoying the leisure life at its very best. The rippling waters, the serenity that surrounds you, offers the greatest relaxation and cleansing of the mind.

"It was in mid-September, 1978, that I caught my 1000th Atlantic salmon out of the Miramichi River. When you consider the fact that the law allows one to catch only two per day, that is rated in fishing circles as an extraordinary feat. I'm mighty proud of it. Also, the fact that I've landed more than 1,000 bonefish is another feat which I look upon with pride. Followers of the legendary Izaak Walton tell me that catching 1,000 or more Atlantic salmon and 1,000 or more bonefish in a life span is comparable to capturing the Triple Crown (batting average, home runs, RBI titles) and the Cy Young Award (the top pitcher in the league) all in one season."

Ron Guidry's 3 Favorite Places To Hunt

In the summer, Yankee lefthander Ron Guidry hunts enemy batters with his blazing fastball and wicked slider, having struck out 1,084 of them in 1,149 innings through the 1982 season. During the fall and winter, Guidry hunts different game. As soon as the baseball season ends, he heads for his home in Lafayette, La., grabs his shotgun, and catches up on his other passion, hunting. He likes the peace and quiet after a long, hard season, preferring to hunt for ducks, and also preferring to stay in the Louisiana country he knows best.

1. Grand Chenier, Cameron Parish, La. (near the Rockefeller Preserve)—duck hunting.
2. Lake Arthur—In the Louisiana bayou country, near where he was born in Lafayette. Guidry takes his whole family here to go duck hunting.

Rifle-armed Ron Guidry is home on the range in Louisiana.

UPI

3. Ron Guidry's Place—This is a secret place in Louisiana where Guidry goes hunting for woodchuck, and he's not about to give away his secret. "Only one other person knows about it," says Guidry. "That's Grandfather Gus, who taught me to hunt when I was a kid."

Reggie Jackson's 12 Most Desirable Automobiles for the Collector

It's not only home runs that the Angels' Reggie Jackson collects. He has a passion for automobiles, which he collects as a hobby and a business. His hobby led him to become automotive editor for *Penthouse* Magazine, for which he writes a monthly column. Jackson owns a Porsche-Audi dealership in California and collects cars, he says, "as a hedge against inflation."

1. Rolls-Royce Corniche with rubber bumper, 1973-77. Value: $85,000*
2. 375 GTB Ferrari Spider, 1973-74. Value: $65,000-$80,000
3. 32 Fudor Phaeton, convertible, open touring car, 1932. Value: $60,000-$70,000
4. Rolls-Royce Corniche, hardtop coupe, 1972-75. Value: $55,000-$70,000*
5. Mercedes-Benz 6.9 four-door sedan, 1976-78. Value: $45,000*
6. Excalibur. Value: $33,000-$36,000
7. Turbo-Carrera Porsche, 1976-78. Value: $35,000*
8. Rolls-Royce Silver Cloud, 1964. Value: $28,000-$35,000
9. Mercedes-Benz 280 SE convertible, 1971. Value: $25,000
10. Mercedes-Benz 280 SL, 1971. Value: $15,000
11. Porsche Speedster 356, 1961. Value: $10,000-$12,000
12. Chevrolet Bel Air, two-door, 1955. Value: $3,000-$5,000*

*Automobiles in Reggie Jackson's collection

7 Pro Football Hall of Famers Who Played Major League Baseball

1. Red Badgro
2. Paddy Driscoll
3. George Halas

Reggie Jackson dangles the keys to the Thunderbird he won as *Sport* Magazine's MVP in the 1977 World Series.

UPI

4. Earle (Greasy) Neale
5. Ernie Nevers
6. Ace Parker
7. Jim Thorpe

Submitted by Dr. Stanley Grosshandler, SABR

11 Major League Baseball Players Who Were Drafted by NFL Teams

1. Sam Chapman, halfback, U. of California, No. 2 draft of Washington Redskins, 1938
2. George (Snuffy) Stirnweiss, halfback, North Carolina, No. 2 draft of Chicago Cardinals, 1940
3. Alvin Dark, halfback, LSU, No. 2 draft of Philadelphia Eagles, 1945
4. Walt Dropo, end, Connecticut, No. 9 draft of Chicago Bears, 1946
5. Lloyd Merriman, halfback, Stanford, No. 3 draft of Chicago Cardinals, 1947
6. Bill Renna, fullback, Santa Clara, No. 12 draft of Los Angeles Rams, 1949
7. Haywood Sullivan, quarterback, Florida, No. 25 draft of Chicago Cardinals, 1953
8. Norm Cash, halfback, Sul Ross State, No. 13 draft of Chicago Bears, 1955
9. Jake Gibbs, quarterback, Mississippi, No. 9 draft of Cleveland Browns, 1961
10. Merv Rettenmund, halfback, Ball State, No. 19 draft of Dallas Cowboys, 1965
11. Dave Winfield, tight end, Minnesota, No. 17 draft of Minnesota Vikings, 1973

Submitted by Jim Campbell, research editor for NFL Properties

14 College Football Hall of Famers Who Made the Majors

1. Charlie Berry, Lafayette College
2. Harry Agganis, Boston University
3. Larry Bettencourt, St. Mary's
4. Paddy Driscoll, Northwestern
5. Paul Giel, Minnesota
6. James Hitchcock, Auburn
7. *Cal Hubbard, Centenary and Geneva
8. Vic Janowicz, Ohio State
9. Ernie Nevers, Stanford
10. Ace Parker, Duke

Jim Thorpe, the Carlisle Indian noted for his Olympic track and field achievements and for football, was also an outfielder in the majors—Giants, Reds, Braves.

UPI

11. Fred Sington, Alabama
12. Jim Thorpe, Carlisle
13. Eric Tipton, Duke
14. Francis Wistert, Michigan

*Hubbard was an umpire.

Submitted by Dr. Stanley Grosshandler, SABR

30 Major League Baseball Players Who Were Outstanding College Basketball Stars

1. Danny Ainge, Brigham Young
2. Ernie Andres, Indiana

Jackie Robinson was UCLA's only four-sport letterman—basketball, track and field, football and baseball.

UCLA-Sports Photo Source

 3. Lou Berger, Maryland
 4. Dave DeBusschere, Detroit
 5. Joe Gibbon, Mississippi
 6. Dick Groat, Duke
 7. Frank Howard, Ohio State
 8. Cotton Nash, Kentucky
 9. Johnny O'Brien, Seattle
10. Dick Ricketts, Duquesne
11. Howie Schultz, Hamline
12. Dave Winfield, Minnesota
13. Gene Conley, Washington State
14. Ron Reed, Notre Dame
15. Rick Herrscher, SMU
16. Jackie Robinson, UCLA
17. Chuck Harmon, Toledo

Dick Groat starred as a Duke cager before embarking on a baseball career as a Pirate shortstop.

Duke-Sports Photo Source

18. Tim Stoddard, North Carolina State
19. Lou Boudreau, Illinois
20. Bob Gibson, Creighton
21. Earl Robinson, California
22. Eddie O'Brien, Seattle
23. Steve Hamilton, Morehead State
24. Sammy White, Washington State
25. John Werhas, USC
26. Don Kessinger, Mississippi
27. Jack Kubiszyn, Alabama
28. Frank Baumholtz, Ohio U.
29. Chuck Connors, Seton Hall
30. Gene Michael, Kent State

Submitted by Rick Obrand, SABR

Stan Isaacs' 10 Hardest License Plates To Come By When on the Road Playing License Plate Games

1. Hawaii
2. Rhode Island
3. North Dakota
4. Alaska
5. Montana
6. Arkansas
7. Idaho
8. Mississippi
9. Wyoming
10. Delaware

X

The Long and the Short

The 3 Longest Baseball Games and the Shortest

1. 33 innings—Pawtucket (R.I.) 3, Rochester, (N.Y.) 2, April 18, 19 and June 23, 1981. The International League contest at Pawtucket, began on the night of April 18 and, after 32 innings, eight hours and seven minutes, the teams were locked in a 2-2 tie. At 4 a.m. on April 19, league president Harold Cooper halted the game. It was postponed until June 23 when Pawtucket first baseman Dave Koza singled home the tie-breaker in the bottom of the 33rd inning.
2. 29 innings—Miami, (Fla.) 4, St. Petersburg (Fla.) 3, June 14, 1966.
3. 26 innings—Brooklyn Dodgers 2, Boston Braves 2, May 2, 1920.

The shortest professional game, in terms of elapsed time, took place on August 30, 1916, according to *The Sporting News*. Winston-Salem was at home against Asheville on the closing day of the Class D North Carolina League season. Since both teams were out of the second-half pennant race and Asheville wanted to catch the late afternoon train home, the managers agreed to an early start and a hurry-up approach.

"We really made a farce of it," said Jack Corbett, the Asheville manager.

"The game had been scheduled at 2 p.m., but got under way at 1:28," according to *The Sporting News* account. "By the time the umpire arrived, about 1:45, the teams already were in the fourth inning. The game wound up at 1:59 (a 31-minute game).

"Each batter swung at the first pitch lobbed over the plate. If a man got a hit and didn't circle the bases, he contrived to keep running to the next base until he was tagged out. Neither side had a runner left on base. To start one inning, Asheville's Doc Lowe pitched before his catcher arrived and the batter singled to center field. When the throw from the outfield came in wild and headed toward the Winston-Salem bench, on-deck hitter Frank Nesser grabbed the ball and threw out his own teammate at second."

Winston-Salem ended up a 2-1 winner and the team made its train.

10 Longest Major League Careers with One Team

1. Brooks Robinson, Baltimore, 23 years
2. Stan Musial, St. Louis, NL, 22 years
3. Al Kaline, Detroit, 22 years
4. Mel Ott, New York, NL, 22 years
5. Cap Anson, Chicago, NL, 22 years
6. Carl Yastrzemski, Boston, AL, 22 years
7. Walter Johnson, Washington, 21 years
8. Ted Lyons, Chicago, AL, 21 years
9. Luke Appling, Chicago, AL, 20 years
10. Red Faber, Chicago, AL, 20 years

Stan Musial spent his entire 22-year Hall-of-Fame career with the Cardinals.
UPI

16 Managers Who Managed the Same Team for 10 or More Consecutive Seasons

Through major league history, teams have employed more than 600 managers, with the average tenure of each manager being closer to Eddie Stanky's one day on the job with the Texas Rangers in 1977 than to Connie Mack's 50 years with the Philadelphia Athletics, which he owned.

1. Connie Mack, Philadelphia Athletics, 50 seasons, 1901-1950.
2. John McGraw, New York Giants, 29 seasons, 1903-1931, plus parts of 1902 and 1932.
3. Walter Alston, Brooklyn and Los Angeles Dodgers, 23 seasons, 1954-1976.

Connie Mack holds the elephant that was the symbol of his beloved A's.
UPI

4. Cap Anson, Chicago (NL), 19 seasons, 1879-1897.
5. Wilbert Robinson, Brooklyn Dodgers, 18 seasons, 1914-1931.
6. Fred Clarke, Pittsburgh, 16 seasons, 1900-1915.
7. Joe McCarthy, New York Yankees, 15 seasons, 1931-1945, plus part of 1946.
8. Earl Weaver, Baltimore Orioles, 14 seasons, 1969-1982, plus part of 1968.
9. Hugh Jennings, Detroit, 14 seasons, 1907-1920.
10. Joe Cronin, Boston Red Sox, 13 seasons, 1935-1947
11. Casey Stengel, New York Yankees, 12 seasons, 1949-1960.
12. Red Schoendienst, St. Louis Cardinals, 12 seasons, 1965-1976.
13. Frank Selee, Boston Beaneaters, 12 seasons, 1890-1901.
14. Miller Huggins, New York Yankees, 12 seasons, 1918-1929, except for 11 games in 1929.
15. Jimmy Dykes, Chicago White Sox, 12 seasons, 1934-1945, except for 17 games in 1934, plus part of 1946.
16. Harry Wright, Philadelphia Phillies, 10 seasons, 1884-1893.

Note: Bill Terry fell short of managing the New York Giants for 10 consecutive seasons. He replaced McGraw 40 games into the 1932 season and remained through 1941.

Furman Bisher's 10 All-Time Baseball Holdouts (Rated on Degree of Stubbornness)

1. Edd Roush: He held out three times, once for an entire season, and still made it to the Hall of Fame.
2. Turkey Mike Donlin: He held out two years in a row, a career record, but spent the time on stage with his wife, Mabel Hite. Otherwise, he would have made it to the Hall of Fame, for he had a lifetime batting average of .333.
3. Frank (Home Run) Baker: He wrote Connie Mack that he should have his contract renegotiated or

forget it, which Mr. Mack promptly did. They both made it to the Hall of Fame.

4. Johnny Kling: Held out and ran a pool room in Kansas City for a whole season. Proving he was right all along, the Cubs won the pennant before his holdout and won again the year he returned, but they did not win while Kling was running his pool room.

5. Heinie Groh: Held out in midseason until Cincinnati sold him to the Giants, whereupon Commissioner Kenesaw Mountain Landis canceled the deal. Poor Heinie, instead of being with a pennant contender, went back to Cincinnati and the second division.

6. Babe Ruth: Held out until Yankee owner Jacob Ruppert agreed to pay him $80,000, which was more than President Herbert Hoover was making. "Hell," cracked the Babe, "I had a better year."

7. Sandy Koufax-Don Drysdale: They win the prize for "team" holdout, each agreeing not to sign with the Dodgers until both were satisfied. As a result, both became $100,000 pitchers.

8. Rufe Gentry: Rocked away the summer of 1945 on his front porch, then when the varsity players came home from the war, he found he had no job.

9. Cliff Bolton: I doubt if he ever really held out. I don't think he ever opened his mail until it was blackberry weather.

10. Bobo Newsom: Always held out just for the exercise. He hated spring training.

10 Major League Players Who Were Less Than Five Feet, Five Inches Tall

1. Eddie Gaedel, 3'7"
2. Nin Alexander, 5'2"
3. Stubby Magner, 5'3"
4. Lou Sylvester, 5'3"
5. Pompeyo (Yo-Yo) Davalillo, 5'3"

6. Monk Cline, 5'4"
7. Doc Gautreau, 5'4"
8. Hugh Nicol, 5'4"
9. Ernie Oravetz, 5'4"
10. Wee Willie Keeler, 5'4½"

Wee Willie Keeler, known for "hitting them where they ain't," had a lifetime average of .345 with the Giants, Brooklyn, Orioles, and New York Highlanders.

UPI

Note: Gaedel was the famous midget who promoter extraordinary Bill Veeck secretly signed to a contract with the St. Louis Browns and sent up as a pinch-hitter against the Detroit Tigers in 1951. Predictably, Gaedel drew a walk.

14 Longest Hitting Streaks by A's Players

1. Bill Lamar, Philadelphia, 1925 29
2. Nap Lajoie, Philadelphia, 1901 28
3. Bing Miller, Philadelphia, 1929 28
4. Doc Cramer, Philadelphia, 1932 28
5. Socks Seybold, Philadelphia, 1901 27
6. Al Simmons, Philadelphia, 1931 27
7. Bob Johnson, Philadelphia, 1934 26
8. Jimmie Foxx, Philadelphia, 1929 24
9. Ferris Fain, Philadelphia, 1952 24
10. Al Simmons, Philadelphia, 1925 23
11. Al Simmons, Philadelphia, 1925 22
12. Doc Cramer, Philadelphia, 1932 22
13. Hector Lopez, Kansas City, 1957 22
14. Vic Power, Kansas City, 1958 22

Baseball's Longest Running Trade Sequence

1933—Frankie Hayes debuts with Philadelphia Athletics.

1944—Hayes, now with St. Louis Browns, is traded back to Philadelphia for Sam Zoldak.

1951—Zoldak goes from Cleveland to Athletics in three-way deal involving Lou Brissie.

1951—Same day, Brissie crosses paths with Minnie Minoso, moving from Cleveland to Chicago.

1957—Minoso is sent to Cleveland in a deal involving Early Wynn.

1948—Wynn went from Washington to Cleveland in a deal involving Eddie Robinson.

1956—Robinson went from Kansas City to Detroit in a deal involving Ned Garver.

1952—Garver had been traded to Detroit in a multi-player trade involving Dick Littlefield.

1957—Littlefield was dealt by the Giants to the Reds for Ray Jablonski.

1954—Jablonski had been traded to the Reds for Frank Smith. Accompanying Jablonski was Gerry Staley.

1961—Staley was traded from Chicago to Kansas City in a deal involving Ray Herbert.

Fireman Sparky Lyle figures in the longest running trade sequence.

UPI

1964—Herbert was traded to Philadelphia for Danny Cater.

1972—Cater was traded from Boston to New York for Sparky Lyle.

1978—Lyle is traded to Texas in a deal involving Juan Beniquez.

1979—Beniquez is traded to Seattle in a deal involving Ruppert Jones.

1981—Jones is traded to San Diego in a deal involving Jerry Mumphrey and John Pacella.

1982—Pacella is traded to Minnesota in a deal involving Roy Smalley.

Submitted by Marty Appel, former Director of Public Relations for the New York Yankees, author of *Baseball's Best: The Hall of Fame Story,* and co-author of *Thurman Munson: An Autobiography.*

Phil. Rizzuto makes a double play throw as routine as ''Holy Cow'' in a
game against the Washington Senators in 1948.

UPI

XI

A Manner of Speaking

Phil Rizzuto's 9 Most Familiar Phrases

Former Yankee shortstop great, Phil Rizzuto, has been the "Voice of the Yankees" since 1957.

1. "Holy Cow."
2. "I wanna tell ya."
3. "That huckleberry."
4. "That's gann . . . way back . . . way back . . . in the upper deck."
5. (After a player has made a great play) "How do ya like that (player's name)? He's unbelievable!"
6. "Tough break for . . ."
7. "Yankees with a golden opportunity here."
8. "He hit that ball nine miles."
9. "The Yankees' lead is (number of) games, but only (number) in the all-important loss column."

SOURCE: *Newsday*

Rosey Rowswell gave Aunt Minnie his home run call.

Ted Patterson Collection

Stan Isaacs' 12 Sportscasters' Bleeding-To-Death Expressions That Drive Stakes into the Hearts of Grammarians

Stan Isaacs is TV and radio sports critic for Long Island's *Newsday*.

1 (tie). "Incredible," "Unbelievable," "Fantastic."
4. "At this point in time."
5. "He's something else."
6. "Some kind of. . . ."
7. "He gave him (all) (more than) he wanted."
8. "Young freshman."
9. "A real (good) (hot) (fine). . . ."
10. "He popped him up."
11 (tie). "Threw caution to the winds," "deadlock."

6 Famous Home Run Calls by Announcers

1. "It's going, going, gone . . ."—Mel Allen
2. "Bye-Bye, Baby."—Russ Hodges
3. "Goodbye, Dolly Grey."—Leo Durocher
4. "Hey, Hey."—Jack Brickhouse
5. "Open the window, Aunt Minnie."—Rosey Rowswell
6. "Kiss it goodbye."—Bob Prince

Yogi Berra's 20 Best Yogi-isms

1. When he was honored at "Yogi Berra Night" in Sportsman's Park, St. Louis: "I want to thank all those who made this night necessary."
2. To a young player who was trying to emulate the batting style of a veteran player: "If you can't imitate him, don't copy him."
3. His philosophy of baseball: "Ninety percent of this game is half mental."
4. On the 1973 pennant race: "It ain't over until it's over."

Russ Hodges was a Giant institution, just like Willie Mays, his guest at a San Francisco broadcast.

San Francisco Giants/Sports Photo Source

5. About a popular Minneapolis restaurant: "Nobody goes there any more, it's too crowded."
6. Explaining why left field is a difficult position to play in Yankee Stadium when shadows fall during a day game in October: "It gets late early out there."
7. On golf: "Ninety percent of the putts that fall short of the cup don't go in."
8. Explaining declining attendance in Kansas City: "If people don't want to come to the ballpark, how are you gonna stop them?"
9. His reason why the Yankees lost the 1960 World Series to the Pittsburgh Pirates: "We made too many wrong mistakes."
10. Explaining why he expected to be a successful rookie manager with the Yankees in 1964 despite having no managerial experience: "You observe a lot by watching."

11. When asked what he does the afternoon of a night game: "I usually take a two-hour nap, from one o'clock to four."

12. In an argument with an umpire who ruled that a ball hit the concrete wall and was in play; Berra said it hit a wooden barricade beyond the fence and, therefore, should be a home run: "Anybody who can't hear the difference between a ball hitting wood and a ball hitting concrete must be blind."

13. To a distraught Billy Martin, who had locked his keys in his Mark V one spring: "You gotta call a blacksmith."

14. To an admirer, who noticed him wearing a different Izod sweater every day and wondered if he has them in all colors: "The only color I don't have is navy brown."

15. To a member of the Yankees' traveling party who entered the lobby of a Chicago hotel and jokingly told Berra he was waiting for Bo Derek: "Well, I haven't seen him."

16. To a friend who said he wanted to go to a particular Fort Lauderdale restaurant, but feared it would be too crowded: "Then why did you wait so long to go now?"

17. To someone who saw Berra at a Yankee party and wondered why he wasn't dancing: "Because I got rubber shoes on."

18. To a sportswriter who complained to Yogi that he just spent the exorbitant amount of $8.95 for a breakfast of juice, coffee and English muffin: "That's because they have to import those English muffins."

19. Upon seeing a well-endowed blonde woman: "Who's that, Dag-wood?"

20. To Joe Altobelli, who was celebrating his 50th birthday: "Now you're an old Italian scallion."

Bob Wolf's 13 Favorite Johnny Logan-isms

Bob Wolf covered the Milwaukee Braves for the Milwaukee *Journal* after the team moved from Boston in 1953. He had the good fortune to cover a pennant-winning team that included Hall of Famers Henry Aaron, Warren

Spahn and Eddie Mathews. But he considers Johnny Logan, the team's outstanding shortstop, one of the most memorable players he covered because of Logan's penchant for the malaprop.

1. When told something he had complained about in the *Journal* was a typographical error: "The hell it was. It was a clean base hit."
2. Upon receiving an award: "I will perish this trophy forever."
3. After seeing "Macbeth" on television: "They've got a new Shakespearean play, 'McBride.' It's got a lot of suspension."
4. Asked to pick the No. 1 baseball player of all time: "I'd have to go with the immoral Babe Ruth."
5. In a speech at a dinner for Stan Musial: "Tonight we're honoring one of the all-time greats of baseball. Stan Musial. He's immoral."
6. To Mrs. Lou Perini aboard the late clubowner's yacht: "You have a very homely yacht."
7. When told about a trade: "Yeah, did you see it on the radio?"
8. Upon being introduced to someone: "I know the name, but I can't replace the face."
9. While dining in a restaurant: "That waitress is all right, but she's unchattable."
10. When the Braves were in a slump: "We're just tiresome, that's all."
11. Discussing the Braves after being traded to Pittsburgh: "They're all right, but they've got too many young youths."
12. On the Braves' rebuilding program: "Rome wasn't born in a day."
13. Ordering dessert: "I'll have pie ala mode with ice cream."

Jerry Coleman's 14 Best (But Not Only) Malaprops

Before he left the broadcasting booth to manage the San Diego Padres, former New York Yankee infield star Jerry Coleman spent almost 20 years announcing the games of the Padres, Yankees and Angels. Coleman is back in the booth again and amusing his listeners with statements like the following:

1. "We're all sad to see Glenn Beckert leave. Before he goes, though, I hope he stops by so we can kiss him good-bye. He's that kind of guy."
2. "On the mound is Randy Jones, the left-hander with the Karl Marx hairdo."
3. "There's a fly ball deep to center field. Winfield is going back, back . . . he hits his head against the wall. It's rolling toward second base."
4. "He slides into second with a standup double."
5. "Rich Folkers is throwing up in the bullpen."
6. "Grubb goes back, back . . . he's under the warning track, and he makes the play."
7. "The big ballpark can do it all."
8. "Young Frank Pastore may have just pitched the biggest victory of 1979, maybe the biggest victory of the year."
9. "If Rose's streak was still intact, with that single to left, the fans would be throwing babies out of the upper deck."
10. "Hrabosky looks fierce in that Fu Manchu haircut."
11. "Bob Davis is wearing his hair different this year, short and with curls, like Randy Jones wears. I think you call it a Frisbee."
12. "Next up for the Cardinals is Barry, Carry, Garry Templeton."
13. "Hendrick simply lost that sun-blown pop-up."
14. "Those amateur umpires are certainly flexing their fangs tonight."

Graig Nettles' 7 Best One-Liners

The Yankees' Gold Glove third baseman is not only quick
with his mitt, he's also quick with his wit. He takes pride
in coming up with the subtle one-liner that best fits the
occasion. His humor is sharp and sarcastic, and sometimes
at his own expense. For example, he has written on the
back of his glove, "E-5," the baseball scorer's shorthand
for "Error-third baseman."

1. On what it's like to play for the Yankees: "Most kids,
   when they're growing up, want to play in the major
   leagues or be in the circus. I'm lucky, I got to do
   both."
2. On the advantages of playing in New York: "You get
   to see Reggie Jackson play every day." On the
   disadvantages of playing in New York: "You get to see
   Reggie Jackson play every day."
3. When former teammate Sparky Lyle was traded the
   year after he won the American League Cy Young
   Award: "Sparky went from Cy Young to Sayonara."
4. Frustrated because he was often placed sixth or seventh
   in the Yankee batting order: "I guess I don't strike out
   enough to bat fourth."
5. Still frustrated at batting sixth or seventh in the Yankee
   batting order: "It's a good thing Babe Ruth isn't still
   here. If he was, George (Steinbrenner) would have him
   bat seventh and say he's overweight."
6. After being fined for missing a "Welcome Home"
   luncheon: "If the Yankees want somebody to play third
   base, they've got me. If they want someone to attend
   banquets, they can get Georgie Jessel."
7. On an airplane trip: "We've got a problem. Luis Tiant
   wants to use the bathroom and it says no foreign ob-
   jects in the toilet."

Harold Rosenthal's 10 Most Memorable Baseball Quotes

As a baseball writer for the defunct New York *Herald-Tribune,* Harold Rosenthal always had a good ear for a quote.

1. "He's dead at the present time."—Casey Stengel, referring to a departed comrade-in-arms.
2. "The road will make a bum of the best of them." —Anonymous. First believed to have been used by Hannibal on his elephant-crossing of the Alps, in his futile attack on Rome.
3. "Don't give him nuthin' good to hit, but don't walk him."—Curious advice given by a harassed manager to a harassed pitcher in a tough situation. First recorded mention came from Harry Wright, manager of Providence the year Old Hoss Radbourne won 60 games.
4. "No one should be able to steal second base on a lefthanded pitcher."—This quote is attributed to Branch Rickey, one of the true geniuses produced by the game. He was talking about the advantages of a left-hander, who always has the runner in view. Rickey said nothing about stealing on right-handed catchers, of which he was one. Catching for the New York Highlanders, he gave up what is still a record of 14 stolen bases in one game. He claimed he had a sore arm that day.
5. "No one was ever paid more than he was worth."— This is a comparatively recent addition, coming after the owners, in their rush to give the store away, started handing out $300,000 salaries to 12-game winners when they became available as free agents. The quote is attributed to pitcher Wayne Garland, who went from the Orioles to the Indians. When he failed to produce, he said: "I didn't ask for the money, they offered it to me. No one was ever paid more than he was worth." The kid's right.
6. "Always take two."—James Parnell Dawson, the late *New York Times* baseball writer, advising a young

writer on how to act when the post-dinner cigars are
handed out.

7. "All the Reds have to do is win one more game each
week to be right in there for the pennant race."—Gabe
Paul when he was boss of the Cincinnati Reds and
they were a chronic second-division club. This is in
the same category as "If my grandmother had a beard
and wore Confederate gray, she'd have been General
Beauregard."

8. "Only half the lies they tell about the Irish are true."
—The late Walter O'Malley, who built an empire that
produced the first three-million attendance ball club,
got tired of people telling him how he had stolen half
of Los Angeles when he moved the Dodgers west-
ward, and used to fall back upon his County Donegal
line to end the discussion. If it hadn't been O'Malley
building a ballpark within howitzer range of downtown City Hall, it probably would have been some
chemical company poisoning the surrounding 350,000
square miles. Instead, the customers got Sandy Koufax,
Don Drysdale and Maury Wills.

9. "Tip half dollars."—Joe DiMaggio in the days when
a quarter tip was a substantial gratuity and ballplayers
were leaving 15-cent tips at dinner.

10. Never underestimate the stupidity of the American
public."—Edward T. Murphy, a pre-World War II
baseball writer in New York, who was upset by the
public's acceptance of the shenanigans and all-around
perfidy of the baseball owners. Murphy quit what
used to be regarded as a highly attractive job as a
traveling baseball writer and went inside to work on
the desk with the advent of night baseball, saying, "I
don't want to sit around like a burglar all day, waiting
for it to get dark so I can go to work."

XII

Hall of Fame

10 Hall of Famers Receiving Highest
Percentage of Votes

	Player	Year	Ballots Cast	Votes	Omitted	Percentage
1.	Ty Cobb	1936	226	222	4	98.2
2.	Henry Aaron	1982	415	406	9	97.8
3.	Honus Wagner	1936	226	215	11	95.1
4.	Babe Ruth	1936	226	215	11	95.1
5.	Willie Mays	1979	432	409	23	94.7
6.	Bob Feller	1962	160	150	10	93.8
7.	Ted Williams	1966	302	282	20	93.4
8.	Stan Musial	1969	340	317	23	93.2
9.	Brooks Robinson	1983	374	344	30	91.9
10.	Christy Mathewson	1936	226	205	21	90.7

Note: In order for a player to be voted into the Hall of Fame, he must be named on 75 percent of the ballots cast by members of the Baseball Writers Association of America, who may list up to 10 names on each annual ballot.

Ty Cobb: Highest of the high in Hall of Fame balloting.

Bill Libby's 7 Shortstops Who Should Be in the Hall of Fame

Bill Libby has written more than 60 books, many of them on baseball. Like many, he decries the lack of shortstops in the Hall of Fame.

"Defense is as important as offense in sports," Libby

Shortstop Pee Wee Reese, one of the Dodger Boys of Summer, starred with the team for nearly 20 years.

UPI

says, "but baseball refuses to recognize it. Many lesser players are in the Hall of Fame while a number of outstanding players at the most important defensive position, shortstop, have been overlooked, as of Feb. 1, 1983. Less than 12 percent of those in the Hall of Fame were shortstops, 12 out of 138, and that includes Ernie Banks, who played much of his career at first base and was picked largely for his offensive skills. But these fellows could hit, too."

1. Phil Rizzuto
2. Pee Wee Reese
3. Marty Marion
4. Luis Aparicio
5. Alvin Dark
6. Johnny Pesky
7. Roy McMillan

Libby adds: "A pretty good case can be made for a number of outstanding defensive second basemen who hit well and helped teams to pennants, and deserve consideration for the Hall of Fame; such as Joe Gordon, Nellie Fox, Bobby Doerr and Red Schoendienst."

Bill Rubinstein's 3 All-Time All-Star Teams of Old Timers Who Should Be in the Hall of Fame but Aren't

Dr. William D. Rubinstein was born in the United States but is now associated with Deakin University's School of Social Sciences in Australia. He is a member of the Society of American Baseball Research.

First Team	Second Team	Third Team
1b—Mickey Vernon	Gil Hodges	Stuffy McInnis
2b—Buddy Myer	Ross Barnes	Tony Lazzeri
3b—Lave Cross	Ray Dandridge	Pee Wee Reese
ss—Arky Vaughn	George Davis	Phil Rizzuto
of—Pete Browning	Bobby Veach	Spots Poles
of—Joe Jackson	Harry Stovey	Ken Williams

of—Babe Herman	Christobel Torriente	Richie Ashburn
c—Ernie Lombardi	Johnny Kling	Biz Mackey
p—Carl Mays	Tony Mullane	Urban Shocker
p—Hal Newhouser	Wes Ferrell	Dick Redding
p—Smokey Joe Williams	Vic Willis	Wilbur Cooper
mgr—Ned Hanlon	Frank Selee	Charlie Grimm

Dr. Rubinstein adds: "All of these players finished their careers before 1964 and thus cannot be considered for enshrinement in the Baseball Writers Association's annual elections, but must hope the Veteran's Committee gets around to noticing their existence.

"Most of these players are well known to experts, but a few are so little known that many fans will never have heard of them, despite their imposing statistics. Stuffy McInnis of the A's $100,000 infield batted .308 lifetime, mainly during the dead ball era, with 2,406 hits. He appeared in five World Series. George Davis, probably the most underrated player in baseball history, was a shortstop for 20 years and batted .297 with 2,688 hits. Lave Cross, probably the best third baseman of his time, hit .292 with 2,644 hits. Ross Barnes was probably the old National Association's outstanding player.

"Dandridge, Mackey, Torriente, Poles, Redding and Joe Williams were great stars of the old Negro Leagues, all of whom were probably the equal of white Hall of Famers of their day. Joe Williams was probably the greatest black pitcher of all time, better than Paige, Gibson or Jenkins. Ty Cobb said he would have been "a sure 30-game winner" in the majors. Ned Hanlon was arguably the greatest manager in history, since as leader of the great Baltimore Orioles of the 1890s, he trained John McGraw, who taught Casey Stengel, who taught Billy Martin. . . .

"Some day, the Veterans Committee may wake up long enough to remember the achievements of these great stars and others like Tony Lazzeri, Cy Williams, George Van Haltren, Jimmy Ryan and Jim Mutrie, who also deserve enshrinement as much as most of the stars already in Cooperstown."

Herman Masin's All-Time Team of Players Who Won an MVP Award but Are Not in the Hall of Fame

1b—Dolph Camilli
2b—Nellie Fox
3b—Ken Boyer
ss—Phil Rizzuto
of—Roger Maris
of—Hank Sauer
of—Jackie Jensen
 c—Ernie Lombardi
 p—Bucky Walters

Herman Masin's All-Time Team of Players Who Are in the Hall of Fame but Never Won an MVP Award

1b—Jim Bottomley
2b—Billy Herman
3b—Eddie Mathews
ss—Luke Appling
of—Goose Goslin
of—Duke Snider
of—Chick Hafey
 c—Al Lopez
 p—Red Ruffing

2 Teams That Did Not Win a Pennant in 1933 Despite Having Four Hall of Famers Pitch for Them*

1. New York Yankees (2nd)—Lefty Gomez, Red Ruffing, Herb Pennock, Babe Ruth.
2. St. Louis Cardinals (5th)—Dizzy Dean, Dazzy Vance, Burleigh Grimes, Jesse Haines.

*Haines, Grimes (both 39) and Vance (42) won 15 games among them. Ruth, 38, won his only start—his second pitching appearance in 13 years—despite giving up 12 hits and five runs.

SOURCE: Frank Kelly

Hank Greenberg makes Golda Meir's team.

UPI

XIII

Name-Calling

All-Time Baseball Teams That Politicians, Statespeople and Other Celebrities Might Have Chosen

"Mr. President, as the nation's No. 1 baseball fan, would you be willing to name your all-time baseball team?"

When President Nixon not only said he would, but did, and made the sports pages of just about every newspaper in the country with his selections, that was an open invitation for everybody to get into the act.

In the interest of fair play, it seems only right that others be given equal time.

What follows are the teams politicians, statespeople and other celebrities might have chosen if they had the time, the inclination, and the opportunity. The selections are hypothetical, but the players chosen are real people who actually played in the major leagues.

Leonid Brezhnev

First base—Lefty O'Doul
Second base—Red Schoendienst
Third base—Red Rolfe
Shortstop—Pinky May
Outfield—Eric (The Red) Tipton
Outfield—Red Murray
Outfield—Lou (The Mad Russian) Novikoff
Catcher—Red Dooin
Pitcher—Lefty Gomez

Don Vito Corleone

First base—Joe Pepitone
Second base—Tony Lazzeri
Third base—Joe Torre
Shortstop—Phil Rizzuto
Outfield—Joe DiMaggio
Outfield—Rocky Colavito
Outfield—Carl Furillo
Catcher—Yogi Berra
Pitcher—Sal Maglie

Frank Buck

First base—Snake Deal
Second base—Nellie Fox
Third base—Possum Whitted
Shortstop—Rabbit Maranville
Outfield—Mule Haas
Outfield—Ox Eckhardt
Outfield—Goat Anderson
Catcher—Doggie Miller
Pitcher—Old Hoss Radbourn

e. e. cummings

first base—r. c. stevens
second base—a. j. mc coy
third base—i. i. mathison
shortstop—j. c. hartman
outfield—g. g. walker
outfield—j. w. porter

outfield—r. e. hildebrand
catcher—j. c. martin
pitcher—w. a. kearns

Golda Meir

First base—Ron Blomberg
Second base—Rod Carew
Third base—Al Rosen
Shortstop—Eddie Feinberg
Outfield—Hank Greenberg
Outfield—Goody Rosen
Outfield—Cal Abrams
Catcher—Joe Ginsberg
Pitcher—Sandy Koufax

Gov. Alfred E. Smith

First base—Willie Smith
Second base—George Smith
Third base—Charlie Smith
Shortstop—Billy Smith
Outfield—Al Smith
Outfield—Reggie Smith
Outfield—Elmer Smith
Catcher—Hal Smith
Pitcher—Al Smith

Jack Jones

First base—Nippy Jones
Second base—Dalton Jones
Third base—Willie (Puddinhead) Jones
Shortstop—Cobe Jones
Outfield—Cleon Jones
Outfield—Ruppert Jones
Outfield—Fielder Jones
Catcher—Bill Jones
Pitcher—Randy Jones

Lyndon Johnson

First base—Deron Johnson
Second base—Don Johnson

Third base—Billy Johnson
Shortstop—Bob Johnson
Outfield—Alex Johnson
Outfield—Lou Johnson
Outfield—Indian Bob Johnson
Catcher—Cliff Johnson
Pitcher—Walter Johnson

Sweet Georgia Brown

First base—Ike Brown
Second base—Jimmy Brown
Third base—Bobby Brown
Shortstop—Larry Brown
Outfield—Ollie Brown
Outfield—Bobby Brown
Outfield—Gates Brown
Catcher—Dick Brown
Pitcher—Mordecai (Three Finger) Brown

Betty Friedan

First base—Mary Calhoun
Second base—Sadie Houck
Third base—She Donahue
Shortstop—Lena Blackburne
Outfield—Gail Henley
Outfield—Baby Doll Jacobson
Outfield—Estel Crabtree
Catcher—Bubbles Hargrave
Pitcher—Lil Stoner

James Beard

First base—Juice Latham
Second base—Peaches Graham
Third base—Pie Traynor
Shortstop—Chico Salmon
Outfield—Soupy Campbell
Outfield—Peanuts Lowrey
Outfield—Oyster Burns
Catcher—Pickles Dillhoefer
Pitcher—Noodles Hahn

J. P. Morgan

First base—Norm Cash
Second base—Don Money
Third base—Milton Stock
Shortstop—Ernie Banks
Outfield—Art Ruble
Outfield—Elmer Pence
Outfield—Bobby Bonds
Catcher—Gene Green
Pitcher—Jim Grant

Norman Vincent Peale

First base—Earl Grace
Second base—Johnny Priest
Third base—Frank Bishop
Shortstop—Angel Hermoso
Outfield—Dave Pope
Outfield—Hi Church
Outfield—Maurice Archdeacon
Catcher—Mickey Devine
Pitcher—Howie Nunn

John Coleman

First base—Sunny Jim Bottomley
Second base—Nippy Jones
Third base—Gene Freese
Shortstop—Stormy Weatherly
Outfield—Hurricane Hazle
Outfield—Curt Flood
Outfield—Icicle Reeder
Catcher—Sun Daly
Pitcher—Windy McCall

Jimmy the Greek

First base—Frank Chance
Second base—Lucky Jack Lohrke
Third base—Charlie Deal
Shortstop—John Gamble
Outfield—Curt Welch
Outfield—Trick McSorley

Hall of Famer Goose Goslin was a farmboy from New Jersey who played outfield for the Senators, the Browns and the Tigers. His ninth-inning single enabled the Tigers to win the 1935 World Series over the Cubs.

UPI

Outfield—Ace Parker
Catcher—Candy LaChance
Pitcher—Shufflin' Phil Douglas

John James Audubon

First base—Andy Swan
Second base—Johnny Peacock
Third base—Jiggs Parrott
Shortstop—Chicken Stanley
Outfield—Ducky Medwick
Outfield—Goose Goslin
Outfield—Bill Eagle
Catcher—Birdie Tebbetts
Pitcher—Robin Roberts

Foster Brooks

First base—Sherry Robertson
Second base—Mickey Finn
Third base—Billy Lush
Shortstop—Bobby Wine
Outfield—Jigger Statz
Outfield—Brandy Davis
Outfield—Half Pint Rye
Catcher—George Gibson
Pitcher—John Boozer

Rand-McNally

First base—Frank Brazill
Second base—Chile Gomez
Third base—Frenchy Bordagaray
Shortstop—Sal Madrid
Outfield—Germany Schaefer
Outfield—Dutch Holland
Outfield—Clyde Milan
Catcher—Dick West
Pitcher—Vinegar Bend Mizell

Queen Elizabeth

First base—Duke Carmel
Second base—Royal Shaw

Third base—Count Campau
Shortstop—John Knight
Outfield—Prince Oana
Outfield—Bris Lord
Outfield—Mel Queen
Catcher—Earl Averill
Pitcher—Clyde King

9 Nicknames That Unfortunately Never Caught On

1. Bruce (Eggs) Benedict
2. Alan (Bananas) Foster
3. Joe (Chicken Catcher) Torre
4. Felipe (Bob) Alou
5. Clyde (Chicken Ala) King
6. Jose (Caribbean) Cruz
7. Doug (Big) Bird
8. Barry (Big) Foote
9. Gene (Half) Nelson

5 Baseball-Playing Palindromes

A palindrome is a word, or name, that reads the same backwards and forwards. In the history of baseball, there have been only five major league players whose last names read the same backwards and forwards.

1. Truck Hannah, New York Yankees, 1918-1920
2. Toby Harrah, Washington Senators, 1971; Texas Rangers, 1972-1978; Cleveland Indians, 1979-
3. Eddie Kazak, St. Louis Cardinals, 1948-1952; Cincinnati Reds, 1952.
4. Dick Nen, Los Angeles Dodgers, 1963; Washington Senators, 1965-1967; Chicago Cubs, 1968.
5. Johnny Reder, Boston Red Sox, 1932.

Ray Fitzgerald's 20 Great Nicknames

The late Ray Fitzgerald, an admitted list junkie, wrote sports lists and great columns for the Boston *Globe*.

1. Joe (Horse Belly) Sargent
2. George (White Wings) Tebeau
3. Harry (Silk Stockings) Schafer
4. Jimmy (The Human Mosquito) Slagle
5. Lou (The Nervous Greek) Skizas
6. Dick (Dr. Strangelove) Stuart
7. Sammy (The Dixie Thrush) Strang
8. Jim (Abba Dabba) Tobin
9. Jim (Little Nemo) Stevens
10. Fred (The People's Cherce) Walker
11. Leon (Daddy Wags) Wagner
12. Harry (Bird Eye) Truby
13. John Francis (Phenomenal) Smith
14. Walter (No Neck) Williams
15. Rollie (Bunions) Zeider
16. Charlie (Swamp Baby) Watson
17. Billy (The Evangelist) Sunday
18. Honus (The Flying Dutchman) Wagner
19. Jim (The Toy Cannon) Wynn
20. Alva (Bear Tracks) Javery

Furman Bisher's 10 All-Time Favorite Minor League Team Nicknames

Furman Bisher, sports editor and sports columnist of the Atlanta *Journal*, is a list maker from way back.

1. Sanford (Fla.) Celeryfeds
2. Lumberton (NC.) Tobacconists
3. Wilmington (Del.) Blue Rocks
4. Zanesville (Ohio) Greys
5. Bisbee (Ariz.) Bees
6. Toledo (Ohio) Mud Hens
7. High Point (NC.) Pointers
8. Lancaster (Pa.) Red Roses

9. York (Pa.) White Roses
10. Springfield (Ill.) Rail-Splitters

Real Names of 37 Well-Known Baseball Players

1.	Ping Bodie	(Francesco Stephano Pezzolo)
2.	Sammy Bohne	(Samuel Arthur Cohen)
3.	Bunny Brief	(Antonio Bordetzki)
4.	Andy Carey	(Andrew Arthur Nordstrom)
5.	Max Carey	(Maximillian Carnarius)
6.	Joe Collins	(Joseph Edward Kollonige)
7.	Stan Coveleski	(Stanislaus Kowalewski)
8.	Frank Demaree	(Joseph Franklin DiMaria)
9.	Johnny Dickshot	(John Arthur Dicksus)
10.	Cozy Dolan	(James Alberts)
11.	Mickey Doolan	(Michael Joseph Doolittle)
12.	Joe Glenn	(Joseph Charles Gurzensky)
13.	Pete Gray	(Peter J. Wyshner)
14.	Eddie Kazak	(Edward Terrence Tkaczuk)
15.	Dick Kokos	(Richard Jerome Kokoszka)
16.	Joe Koppe	(Joseph Kopchia)
17.	Dave Koslo	(George Bernard Koslowski)
18.	Sandy Koufax	(Sanford Braun)
19.	Ed Levy	(Edward Charles Whitner)
20.	Eddie Lopat	Edmund Walter Lopatynski)
21.	Connie Mack	(Cornelius Alexander McGillicuddy)
22.	Ray Mack	(Raymond James Mickovsky)
23.	Lee Magee	(Leopold Christopher Hoernschmeyer)
24.	Duke Markell	(Harry Duquesne Marowsky)
25.	Babe Martin	(Boris Michael Martinovich)
26.	Billy Martin	(Alfred Manuel Pesano)
27.	Eddie Mayo	(Edward Joseph Mayoski)
28.	Charlie Metro	(Charles Moreskonich)
29.	Cass Michaels	(Casimir Eugene Kwietniewski)
30.	Erv Palica	(Ervin Walter Pavliecivich)
31.	Johnny Pesky	(John Michael Paveskovich)
32.	Tony Piet	(Anthony Francis Pietruska)
33.	Babe Pinelli	(Rinaldo Angelo Paolinelli)
34.	Jimmy Reese	(James Hymie Soloman)

Sandy Koufax, who went from the University of Cincinnati to the Brooklyn Dodgers, was born Sanford Braun.

UPI

35. Al Simmons   (Aloysius Harry Szymanski)
36. Hal Trosky   (Harold Arthur Troyavesky)
37. Whitey Witt   (Ladislaw Waldemar Wittkowski)

10 Members of a Workmanlike Pitching Staff with 2 Catchers and 1 Manager

Pitchers:
1. Steve Barber
2. Max Butcher
3. Bob Carpenter
4. Mort Cooper
5. Nelson Potter
6. Hal Schumacher
7. Phenomenal Smith
8. Clyde Wright
9. Ed Farmer
10. Stu Miller

Catchers:
1. Bill Plummer
2. Darrell Porter

Manager:
1. Earl Weaver

Pat McDonough's All-Time Team of People Named Williams.

Pat McDonough was one of the early figger filberts on the New York *World-Telegram*.

1b—Billy Williams
2b—Davey Williams
3b—Dick Williams
ss—Dib Williams
of—Ted Williams
of—Ken Williams
of—Cy Williams
c—Earl Williams
p—Lefty Williams
p—Stan Williams
mgr—Dick Williams

Note: A powerful outfield. All three Williamses led their league in home runs at one time or another.

Pat McDonough's All-Time Team of Presidential Namesakes

   1b—Chuck Harrison
   2b—Horace Ford
   3b—Ed Grant
   ss—Travis Jackson
   of—Hack Wilson
   of—Shoeless Joe Jackson
   of—Reggie Jackson
    c—Gary Carter
    p—Walter Johnson
    p—Babe Adams
    p—Whitey Ford
    p—Reggie Cleveland
    p—Jim Grant

George Gipe's 20 Favorite Old-Time Major League Baseball Teams with Unusual Nicknames

1. Fort Wayne Kekiongas (National Association, 1871)
2. Elizabeth Resolutes (National Association, 1873)
3. Middletown Mansfields (National Association, 1872)
4. Cleveland Spiders (National League, 1879-84, 1889-99)
5. Boston Beaneaters (National League, 1883-1906)
6. Boston Doves (National League, 1907-08)
7. Boston Pilgrims (National League, 1909-11)
8. Brooklyn Bridegrooms (National League, 1890-98)
9. Chicago Orphans (National League, 1898)
10. Boston Somersets (American League, 1901-04)
11. Boston Puritans (American League, 1905-06)
12. Cleveland Molly McGuires (American League, 1912-14)
13. Chicago Whales (Federal League, 1914-15)
14. St. Louis Terriers (Federal League, 1914-15)
15. Baltimore Terrapins (Federal League, 1914-15)
16. Newark Peppers (Federal League, 1915)
17. Brooklyn Tip-Tops (Federal League, 1914-15)

18. Brooklyn Wonders (Players' League, 1890)
19. Pittsburgh Burghers (Players' League, 1890)
20. Troy Haymakers (National Association, 1871-72)

29 Famous Baseball Batteries Made Up of Pitchers and Catchers Who, Unfortunately, Never Played Together, but Did, in Fact, Play in the Major Leagues and Only Chance Prevented Us from Hearing the Public Address Announcer Say, "The Battery for Today's Game . . ."

1. East and West
2. Johnson and Johnson
3. Holly and Ivie
4. Barnes and Noble
5. Hand and Foote
6. Burns and Allen
7. Black and White
8. Butcher and Baker
9. Nixon and Agnew
10. Kennedy and Johnson
11. Lewis and Clark
12. Rogers and Hart
13. Gilbert and Sullivan
14. Franklin and Marshall
15. Hale and Hardy
16. Bell and Howell
17. Mason and Dixon
18. Masters and Johnson
19. Black and Decker
20. More and Moore
21. Blue and Grey
22. Queen and King
23. High and Lowe
24. Reid and Wright
25. Short and Long
26. Stanley and Livingston
27. Martin and Lewis
28. Rowan and Martin
29. Olsen and Johnson

XIV

The Hot Stove League

2 Presidents Who Did Not Throw Out the First Ball On Opening Day

1. Jimmy Carter
2. Ronald Reagan

It all began when President William Howard Taft attended the season's opener between the Washington Senators and Philadelphia Athletics in 1910. As an added touch, Taft tossed out the first ball from his box seat and launched what was to become a Presidential ritual.

In the days when there was a major league team in Washington, the President could have his lunch at the White House, then motor over to Griffith Stadium or Robert F. Kennedy Stadium and make his pitch. When baseball left the capitol in 1972, Presidents Nixon and Ford kept the streak going by doing their fling on the road. But affairs of state kept President Carter off the first-ball mound during his tenure. As governor of Georgia, he had tossed opening pitches for the Atlanta Braves.

President Franklin D. Roosevelt throws out the first ball to open the 1937 season at Griffith Stadium, Washington. At left is Clark Griffith, owner of the Senators; Connie Mack owner-manager of the A's, is on the other side of the President and the manager is Bucky Harris of the Senators.

UPI

A would-be assassin's bullet canceled President Reagan's pitching assignment in Cincinnati in 1981, but chances are the man who portrayed Grover Cleveland Alexander in *The Winning Team* will throw one before he turns in his seal.

8 Managers Who Won 100 Games in a Season and Lost 100 in Another

1. Leo Durocher, Brooklyn and Chicago (NL)
2. Charlie Dressen, Brooklyn and Washington
3. Gil Hodges, Washington and New York (NL)
4. Bill McKechnie, Boston (NL) and Cincinnati
5. Connie Mack, Philadelphia (AL)
6. Ralph Houk, New York (AL) and Detroit
7. Bill Carrigan, Boston (AL)
8. Casey Stengel, New York (AL) and New York (NL)

Note: Durocher, Dressen, Hodges and Houk all made it in New York and lost it elsewhere. Stengel hit each end of the century double in New York. Dressen experienced the quickest turnaround. Fired by Branch Rickey after winning 105 games for Brooklyn in 1953, he went to Washington two years later and lost 101. Carrigan (with the 1915 and

1927 Red Sox) and Mack are the only managers to have won and lost 100 with the same team. Connie's Philadelphia A's had 100 wins five times, 100 defeats seven times. Hodges and McKechnie are the only ones to have lost 100 before winning 100.

SOURCE: Frank Kelly

26 White Sox and Cubs Managers and/or Head Coaches with Whom Jerome Holtzman Has Traveled

In his more than 30 years on the baseball beat, Jerome Holtzman of the *Chicago Tribune* has survived many managerial changes, including the 1950s Cubs' experiment in which the team was handled by a committee of coaches.

1. Bill Adair
2. Joe Amalfitano
3. Lou Boudreau
4. Harry Craft
5. Larry Doby
6. Leo Durocher
7. Lee Elia
8. Herman Franks
9. Preston Gomez
10. Charlie Grimm
11. Don Gutteridge
12. Vedie Himsl
13. Bob Kennedy
14. Don Kessinger
15. Lou Klein
16. Tony LaRussa
17. Bob Lemon
18. Whitey Lockman
19. Al Lopez
20. Jim Marshall
21. Charlie Metro
22. Paul Richards
23. Bob Scheffing

24. Eddie Stanky
25. Chuck Tanner
26. Elvin Tappe

25 Major Leaguers Who Were Born in Europe

1. Honest John Anderson—Sasbourg, Norway
2. Jimmy Archer—Dublin, Ireland
3. Rugger Ardizoia—Oleggio, Italy
4. Jimmy Austin—Swansea, Wales
5. Heinz Becker—Berlin, Germany
6. Bob Belloir—Heidelberg, Germany
7. Reno Bertoia—St. Vito Uldine, Italy
8. Hank Biasetti—Beano, Italy
9. Bert Blyleven—Zeist, Holland
10. Dave Brain—Hereford, England
11. Al Campanis—Kos, Greece
12. Moe Drabowsky—Ozanna, Poland
13. Olaf Hendriksen—Kirkerup, Denmark
14. Otto Hess—Berne, Switzerland
15. Kurt Krieger—Traisen, Austria
16. Axel Lindstrom—Gustafsburg, Sweden
17. John Michaelson—Tivalkoski, Finland
18. Fritz Mollwitz—Kolberg, Germany
19. Marino Pieretti—Lucca, Italy
20. Rube Schauer—Odessa, Russia
21. Harry Smith—Yorkshire, England
22. Bobby Thomson—Glasgow, Scotland
23. Elmer Valo—Ribnik, Czechoslovakia
24. Jimmy Walsh—Killila, Ireland
25. Jimmy Wiggs—Trondhjeim, Norway

Frank Kelly's 7 Fourth (also Second and Third) Wheels

Frank Kelly is a sports historian who counts wheels when he isn't editing copy in the sports department of the New York *Daily News*.

1. Harry Steinfeldt—The third baseman for the Chicago Cubs' pennant winners in 1906-08, he has been ignored

except as the answer to a trivia question ("Who was the third baseman with Tinker-to-Evers-to-Chance?") This despite leading the Cubs to victory in the 1907 World Series with a .471 average, leading the club in RBI in 1906 (tying for the NL lead) and 1907 and outhitting all three of his Hall of Fame infield mates in 1906. He also had higher fielding averages in 1906 and 1907 than either Johnny Evers or Joe Tinker.

2. Adam Comorosky—The man who played the most seasons (four) in the same outfield with Pittsburgh Hall of Famers Paul and Lloyd Waner, batting .321 and .313 the first two seasons (1929-30).

3. and 4. Andy Cohen and Hughie Critz—From 1925 to 1927, the New York Giants had four future Hall of Famers in their starting infield. The next three seasons, they had three, the outsiders being second basemen Cohen (1928-29) and Critz (1930). Interestingly, Hall of Famers Bill Terry (1b), Travis Jackson (ss) and Fred Lindstrom (3b) played with five different second-base regulars in those six seasons. The others were fellow "immortals" George Kelly (1925), Frankie Frisch (1926) and Rogers Hornsby (1927).

5. and 6. Joe Jackson and Ty Cobb—The only two players to hit over .400 and not win the batting championship. Jackson (.408) was runnerup to Cobb (.420) in 1911, and the Georgia Peach (.401) finished second to George Sisler (.420) in 1922. Poor Shoeless Joe hit .395 in 1912, thus giving him the second-best set of consecutive seasons, average-wise, in American League history. Unfortunately for him, Cobb was having the best back-to-back years (.420 and .410).

7. Bill Voiselle—The No. 3 starter for the pennant-winning Boston Braves in 1948, he was indirectly maligned by the famous slogan about their pitching rotation, "Spahn and Sain, then pray for rain." Actually, Voiselle (13-13 and 3.63) won only two fewer games than Warren Spahn (15-12 and 3.71) and had a lower ERA. But, like Steinfeldt, his name wasn't suitable for rhyming.

9 Big Leaguers Signed by Bots Nekola

A star pitcher at Holy Cross College, Bots Nekola later played in the big leagues with the New York Yankees and Detroit Tigers in the early 1930s. His career came to an end when he was hit in the head by a bat that slipped out of the hands of a hitter, resulting in the loss of sight in Nekola's right eye. That didn't keep him from becoming one of the best spotters of talent. As a scout for the Boston Red Sox for three decades, his territory was the metropolitan region of New York. His most celebrated discovery was Carl Yastrzemski, a Long Island lad whom Bots signed as a shortstop off the campus of Notre Dame in 1958.

1. Carl Yastrzemski
2. Rico Petrocelli
3. Jerry Casale
4. Ken Aspromonte
5. Charlie Schilling
6. Ben Oglivie
7. John Curtis
8. Joe Lahoud
9. Mike Nagy

5 Most Frequently Traded Players

1. Bobo Newsom—16 times
2. Tommy Davis—11 times
3. John Joseph Doyle—10 times
4. Deacon McGuire—10 times
5. Bob Miller—10 times

SOURCE: Philadelphia *Inquirer*

10 Major Leaguers Who Were Born in Colorado

1. Rich (Goose) Gossage, Colorado Springs
2. John Stearns, Denver

Carl Yastrzemski takes a good bite at Yankee Stadium in 1967, a glorious year for the pennant-winning Red Sox and for MVP Yaz.

UPI

3. Tippy Martinez, La Junta
4. Johnny Lindell, Greeley
5. Roy Hartzell, Golden
6. Tom Hughes, Coal Creek
7. Gene Packard, Colorado Springs
8. Dave LaRoche, Colorado Springs
9. Larry Harlow, Colorado Springs
10. Bert Niehoff, Louisville

SOURCE: Larry Bortstein

4 Towns in North Dakota Whose Names Are Associated with Baseball, but Were Not Named After Baseball

1. Alexander, ND
2. Cartwright, ND
3. Cooperstown, ND
4. Donnybrook, ND

Note: Alexander Cartwright was the Father of Modern Baseball and laid out the first baseball diamond. Alexander, ND, was named after the town's founder, a businessman. Cartwright, ND, was named for the first settler-trapper there. The Baseball Hall of Fame is in Cooperstown, NY, but Cooperstown, ND, was named for two brothers who founded the town. A donnybrook is the term used to describe a baseball brawl, but Donnybrook, ND, was named for a town in Ireland.

Submitted by Anthony Cusher, SABR

The Last Active Players for Each of 10 Teams That Moved to Another City

Team	Year Moved	Last Player Active
1. Brooklyn Dodgers, 1957		Don Drysdale, 1969
2. New York Giants, 1957		Willie Mays, 1973
3. Boston Braves, 1953		Eddie Mathews, 1968

Don Drysdale won 209 games with the Brooklyn and Los Angeles Dodgers.

UPI

4. Milwaukee Braves, 1965	Phil Niekro, 1982
5. St. Louis Browns, 1953	Don Larsen, 1967
6. Kansas City Athletics, 1967	Reggie Jackson, Rick Monday, Joe Rudi, 1982
7. Washington Senators, 1960	Jim Kaat, 1982
8. Washington Senators, 1971	Toby Harrah, Del Unser, Larry Biittner, Aurelio Rodriguez, Len Randle, Jeff Burroughs, 1982
9. Seattle Pilots, 1969	Fred Stanley, 1982
10. Philadelphia Athletics, 1954	Vic Power, 1965

Submitted by Marty Appel

17 Men Who Played for Two Separate Franchises in a One-Team City

1. Moe Drabowsky, Kansas City A's and Royals
2. Aurelio Monteagudo, Kansas City A's and Royals
3. Ken Sanders, Kansas City A's and Royals
4. Dave Wickersham, Kansas City A's and Royals
5. Felipe Alou, Milwaukee Braves and Brewers
6. Hank Aaron, Milwaukee Braves and Brewers
7. Phil Roof, Milwaukee Braves and Brewers
8. Rudy Hernandez, Washington Senators, original and expansion
9. Hector Maestri, Washington Senators, original and expansion
10. Don Mincher, Washington Senators, original and expansion
11. Camilo Pascual, Washington Senators, original and expansion
12. Pedro Ramos, Washington Senators, original and expansion
13. Roy Sievers, Washington Senators, original and expansion
14. Johnny Schaive, Washington Senators, original and expansion
15. Zoilo Versalles, Washington Senators, original and expansion
16. Hal Woodeshick, Washington Senators, original and expansion.
17. Diego Segui, Seattle Pilots and Mariners

Note: Special mention goes to Whitey Herzog and Dick Howser (Kansas City), Del Crandall (Milwaukee) and Jim Lemon and Mickey Vernon (Washington), who played for the old franchise and managed the new one.

SOURCE: Frank Kelly

7 Running Members of the Go-Go White Sox

Back in the 1950s, the Chicago White Sox dazzled the baseball world with a team that ran the basepaths with abandon at a time when most teams sat back and waited for the home run. They led the American League in steals every year from 1951 through 1961, thus earning the nickname "Go-Go White Sox."

		Years with Sox	Steals
1.	Luis Aparicio	1956-1961	238
2.	Minnie Minoso	1951-1957, 1960-1961	171
3.	Jim Rivera	1952-1961	154
4.	Jim Landis	1957-1961	95
5.	Nellie Fox	1951-1961	68
6.	Jim Busby	1951, 1955	38
7.	Chico Carrasquel	1951-1955	29

Note: Aparicio led the American League in steals from 1956 through 1961; Minoso led the league from 1951 through 1953; Rivera led the league in 1955.

Submitted by Phil Erwin, SABR

Jack Lang's 9 Major Leaguers Who Made It Despite Physical Deformities

A baseball writer for almost four decades and long-time Secretary-Treasurer of the Baseball Writers Assn. of America, Jack Lang of the New York *Daily News* has no infirmities to which he will admit.

1. Ewell Blackwell—one kidney.
2. Bert Sheppard—one leg.
3. Catfish Hunter—nine toes.
4. Dummy Hoy—mute.
5. Tom Sunkel—one eye.
6. Pete Gray—one arm.
7. Carlos May—no thumb, right hand.
8. Mordecai Brown—three fingers on pitching hand.
9. Lou Johnson—missing half of one ear.

Note: "The perfect man to cover this team," says Lang, "is Tommy Holmes, who had one arm and wrote baseball for many years."

Pete Gray hits away against the Yankees.

UPI

Barry Janoff's New York Yankee Anniversaries in the Month of May

May 1—Babe Ruth's first home run as a Yankee, 1920
May 2—End of Lou Gehrig's consecutive game streak at
    2,130 games, 1939
May 3—Birthday of Charles (Red) Ruffing, 1904
May 4—Birthday of Earle Combs, 1899

The St. Louis Browns' Pete Gray warms up at Yankee Stadium in 1945.

UPI

May 5—Yankee Stadium construction begins, 1922
May 6—Birthday of Dick Wakefield, 1921
May 7—Birthday of Gary Cooper, who portrayed Lou
       Gehrig in the movie, "Pride of the Yankees,"
       1901
May 8—Birthday of Art Lopez, 1937
May 9—Birthday of John Kennedy, 1941
May 10—Birthday of Edward Barrow, 1868
May 11—Birthday of Fred Frazier, 1951
May 12—Birthday of Yogi Berra, 1925
May 13—Birthday of Juan Beniquez, 1950
May 14—Birthday of Dick Howser, 1937
May 15—Start of Joe DiMaggio's 56-game hitting streak,
        1941
May 16—Birthday of Billy Martin, 1928
May 17—Birthday of Carlos May, 1948
May 18—Birthday of Reggie Jackson, 1946
May 19—Birthday of Rick Cerone, 1954
May 20—Birthday of Bobby Murcer, 1946
May 21—Birthday of Bobby Cox, 1941
May 22—Birthday of Tommy John, 1943
May 23—Birthday of Bill Drescher, 1941
May 24—Birthday of Bobby Brown, 1954
May 25—End of Babe Ruth's slugging career when he hits
        last three home runs, for Boston vs. Pittsburgh,
        1935
May 26—Rick Cerone's first career grand slam, 1980
May 27—End of Yankees' intra-city rivalry with permission
        granted to Brooklyn Dodgers and New York
        Giants to move to California
May 28—Birthday of Bob Kuzava, 1923
May 29—Birthday of George McQuinn, 1909
May 30—Birthday of Lou McEvoy, 1902
May 31—Birthday of Tippy Martinez, 1950

30 People Who Quit the Yankees Since George Steinbrenner Bought the Team in 1973

1. Michael Burke
2. Howard Berk
3. Lee MacPhail
4. Bob Fishel
5. Ralph Houk
6. Marty Appel
7. Al Rosen
8. Tal Smith

9. Clyde Kluttz
10. George Pfister
11. Gabe Paul
12. Pat Nugent
13. Pat Gillick
14. Elliot Wahle
15. Dr. Sidney Gaynor
16. Bobby Cox
17. Mickey Morabito
18. Joseph A. W. Iglehart
19. Rob Franklin
20. Jerry Waring
21. Larry Wahl
22. Francis J. (Steve) O'Neill
23. Herman Schneider
24. Joe Garagiola, Jr.
25. Dick Howser (?)
26. Mike Ferraro
27. Joe Altobelli
28. Birdie Tebbetts
29. Ed Broderick
30. Irv Kaze

Note: Rather than admitting this is a source of embarrassment to him, Steinbrenner insists it is a tribute to the Yankees that other clubs hire away his people. "Most of the people who left me went to bigger jobs," he says, citing Lee MacPhail, American League president; Bobby Cox, Mike Ferraro and Joe Altobelli, who left as Yankee coaches to manage other teams; and Gabe Paul, Tal Smith and Pat Gillick, who left the Yankees to become front office chiefs for the Indians, Astros and Blue Jays.

Pete Enich's 30 Baseball Facts of Questionable Value

Pete Enich is director of public relations for the city of Kansas City, Kansas, and a master of sports trivia.

1. A catcher will bend his knees 300 times in a typical doubleheader.

2. The game of polo was never played at the Polo Grounds, home of the New York Giants and the New York Mets prior to the construction of Shea Stadium.

3. Ty Cobb ran 99 miles as a baserunner during his career.

4. According to the Seiko Time Co., baseball's two-millionth run will be scored on June 12, 2042.

5. Fifteen-year-old pitcher Joe Nuxhall retired two of the first three St. Louis Cardinal batters he faced on June 12, 1944, and did not record his third major league out until 1952, eight years later.

6. No major league player with a last name starting with either "I" or "U" has ever hit more than 100 career home runs.

7. Only eight pitchers in major league history won as many games as Cy Young lost.

8. Pete Rose plans to break Ty Cobb's hit record on May 15, 1984.

9. The geometry of baseball indicates that 26½ feet of the 180 feet on the basepaths is unguarded, therefore one ball out of every 6 and 4/25 hit on the ground should be safe.

10. The 1952 Pittsburgh Pirates had the shortest infield in major league history, averaging 5-6¼.

11. Pitcher Art Herring had the smallest feet in major league history—size 3.

12. Johnny Cooney played in the major leagues for 16 full seasons before hitting his first home run.

13. Season tickets were first sold by the National League's Hartford club in 1876.

14. Harmon Killebrew played his entire career, 8,147 at-bats, without one successful sacrifice bunt.

15. The New York Yankees and the Kansas City A's averaged at least two trades a year with each other between 1955 and 1967.

16. Charley (Red) Barrett, pitching for the Boston Braves on August 10, 1944, shut out Cincinnati, 2-0, using only 58 pitches, or 6.44 pitches per inning.

17. Morganna, the Kissing Bandit, made her debut at RFK Stadium in Washington during the 1970 Presidential opener. Frank Howard was her target.

18. In 1932, the entire National League, including pitchers, had a combined batting average of .303.

Poor Harmon Killebrew. He couldn't bunt, but he hit 573 home runs. He poled his 500th and 501st for the Twins in 1971 against the Orioles.

UPI

19. With the exception of Philadelphia-Detroit outfielder Barney McCosky, Bob Feller struck out every opposing American League player who played regularly during the 1946 season.

20. A baseball hit 400 feet has twice as much destructive energy as a bullet fired from a .38 calibre pistol.

21. Assuming that the average home run travels 340 feet, Hank Aaron's career totals traveled 48.61 miles.

22. Some 150 fan letters reached Ty Cobb each month requesting his autograph. Many letters enclosed return-mail stamps. Cobb used the stamps for his own outgoing mail. He burned the fan letters.

23. The minimum major league salary in 1958 was $7,500.

24. Hugh Duffy received a $12.50-a-month raise after hitting .438 in 1894.

25. Ted Klusewski's swing was clocked at 115 mph.

26. Catching a fly ball in one hand, transferring the ball to the throwing hand and releasing the throw takes 9/10 of a second. Catching the ball with two hands, which puts the throwing hand on the ball immediately, takes only 4/10 of a second.

27. When Joe DiMaggio's hitting streak ended at 56 consecutive games in 1941, it cost him $10,000 because the Heinz 57 officials were ready to make a deal with him after the game.
28. The first pinch-hitter in National League history was Jack Doyle, who stepped into a game for Cleveland on June 7, 1892, and promptly singled.
29. It is estimated that Hall of Fame pitcher Warren Spahn won at least 50 games during his career with his bat, hitting away and bunting.
30. Dr. Lyman Briggs, director emeritus for the National Bureau of Standards, claims it is possible for a baseball to curve as much as 17½ inches.

25 Incredibly Tough Trivia Questions
Answers on page 224-225

1. Once, and only once, a major league team and all its players had the same batting averages after a game as before. Explain.
2. Babe Ruth hit one minor league home run. In what city?
3. In 1904 this St. Louis Cardinal pitcher achieved an amazing record for complete games. He started 39 games for the Redbirds and completed every one of them. Name him.
4. What former University of Missouri athlete once struck out Babe Ruth 10 times in a row and 19 out of 31 at bats?
5. What former major league baseball figure was the co-owner of the film rights to "Gone With the Wind?"
6. How did the 1970 Pittsburgh pitching staff compare to a butcher shop?
7. Who was the first rookie to lead the National League in home runs?
8. Who was the first baseball player to use a glove?
9. The first run ever scored against the hapless New York Mets came in a most appropriate fashion. Explain.
10. The story of Johnny Unitas' rise from sandlot football to the NFL is now legendary. He played for the

semipro Bloomfield Rams in 1955 before leading the Baltimore Colts to world championships in 1958 and 1959. What former major league pitcher did Unitas beat out for the quarterback position for the minor league Rams in 1955?

11. Who got four hits in his first major league game and then never played in another?

12. Whose only hit in the majors was a home run?

13. Who led the American League in batting for four consecutive odd-numbered years and then, after failing to lead the fifth consecutive odd year, was sold?

14. One player, from 1971 to 1980, hit over .300 every even year and under .300 every odd year. Who was it?

15. What was the final score of the earliest recorded East Coast baseball game?

16. Who established a new record by losing three World Series games while trying not to?

17. Who were the only brothers in baseball to win batting titles?

18. Who were the only pitching brothers to win the Cy Young Award?

19. Which family had more baseball players than any other?

20. Who were the only brothers to hurl no-hitters?

21. Who were the only players with 3,000 career hits to own lifetime batting averages of under .300?

22. What pitcher won 20 games in his first year in the majors and never pitched again?

23. Who were the only four in baseball history with 3,000 career hits to also hit more than 400 home runs?

24. Who was the only man to hit 30 home runs and steal 30 bases in a season five times?

25. Who are the only men to win batting titles while playing for two different teams during the season?

Submitted by Pete Enich

Answers

1. The 1940 Chicago White Sox were victims of Bob Feller's no-hitter on opening day. Players and team were batting .000 before and after.
2. Toronto, Canada.
3. John Taylor (20-19)
4. Hubert (Shucks) Pruett, St. Louis Browns, 1922-24, who had a career record of 29-48.
5. New York Mets owner Joan Whitney Payson, who, along with her brother, Jock Whitney, owned the 1939 film classic.
6. Three of the Pirate hurlers that year were (Bob) Moose, (Bob) Veale and (John) Lamb.
7. Harry Lumley of Brooklyn, who hit nine in 1904.
8. Charles C. Waite, first baseman for the National Association's Boston Club in 1875.
9. The Mets' first regular-season game was on April 11, 1962, against the St. Louis Cardinals. Pitcher Roger Craig committed a balk in the first inning, allowing Bill White to score from third, opening the door for a season of errors, miscues, tragi-comedy and 120 defeats.
10. Ed Rakow, former hurler for the Dodgers, A's, Tigers and Braves.
11. Roy Jansen of the St. Louis Browns, September 30, 1910.
12. Ron Allen of the St. Louis Cardinals, brother of Hank Allen and Richie Allen, who got one hit in 11 times at bat during the 1972 season.
13. Harry Heilmann of the Detroit Tigers. He averaged .394 in 1921, .403 in 1923, .393 in 1925, and .398 in 1927. In 1929, he averaged "only" .344 and then was sold to Cincinnati.
14. Bill Buckner of the Dodgers and Cubs. He broke his streak in 1981 by hitting .311.
15. The New York Nine beat the New York Knickerbockers, 23-1 in four innings, June 19, 1846.
16. Unlike Chicago's Claude (Lefty) Williams, who "threw" the games during the 1919 "Black Sox" scandal, New York Yankee George Frazier was doing his best when he lost three games during the 1981 series against the Dodgers.

17. Dixie Walker of the Brooklyn Dodgers (.357 in 1944) and Harry Walker of the St. Louis Cardinals and Philadephia Phillies (.363 in 1947).

18. Gaylord and Jim Perry; Gaylord for the American League in 1972 (Cleveland Indians) and again in 1978 for the National League (San Diego Padres); Jim for the American League in 1970 (Minnesota Twins).

19. Five Delahanty brothers played in the majors. The most famous of the five was "Big Ed" Delahanty (1888-1903), elected to the Hall of Fame in 1945; his less famous brothers were Tom Delahanty (1894-97); Jim Delahanty (1901-15); Joe Delahanty (1907-09) and Frank (Pudgie) Delahanty (1905-15).

20. Bob Forsch of the Cardinals (April 16, 1978) and Ken Forsch of the Astros a year later (April 7, 1979).

21. Carl Yastrzemski (.286) and Lou Brock (.292).

22. Henry Schmidt, who was 21-13 for Brooklyn in 1903.

23. Stan Musial (3,630/475), Willie Mays (3,283/660), Hank Aaron (3,771/755), and Carl Yastrzemski (3,318/442 through 1982).

24. Bobby Bonds. While with the Giants, twice, in 1969 (32 HR, 45 SB) and 1973 (39-43); with the Yankees in 1975 (32-30); with the California Angels in 1977 (37-41) and with the Texas Rangers and Chicago White Sox in 1978 (31-43).

25. Harry (The Hat) Walker, who was traded by the St. Louis Cardinals to the Philadelphia Phillies after 10 games of the 1947 season and wound up leading the National League with a .363 batting average, and Dale Alexander, who was traded from the Detroit Tigers to the Boston Red Sox after 23 games in 1932 and went on to lead the American League with a .367 mark.